Praise for

Cicatrizing the Daughters

Cicatrizing the Daughters is a return to everything that is still there, somehow, long after you've left and changed and loved and hurt and grown and shrunk. Sam Moe paves a map for you to get lost in—old haunts become new again, and buildings long forgotten or abandoned twist into things freshly wounded and remembered. This collection will hold your hand and walk you through the depths of memories and feelings you couldn't remember otherwise—sandwiches kept warm in coats, the 1 train, awnings and bodega cats in New York City, the ocean wrapped around past loves, and the ghosts that still live in the kitchen.

—**(re)becca meier**, author of *small wings*

Sam Moe skillfully navigates the crashing waves of traumatic memory in this dynamic collection of vivid prose poems and hybrid work. Her dynamic work expands in the reader's psyche and excites, full of melancholy musings and longing for a connection with patience, love and peace. A striking book!

—**Jose Hernandez Diaz**, author of *Bad Mexican, Bad American*

In Moe's collection *Cicatrizing the Daughters*, Moe positions her love for family, friends and lovers as one of inquiry and arrest. A love letter to mothers, fathers, past lovers, and New York City, Moe writes of unrequited love with a requited understanding and confidence that no matter the meaning or understanding of love, it is enough to just love. In such a beautiful and tender collection, Moe's resolve is found in kitchens, bedrooms, and eating fruit with loved ones who are there and those who aren't.

—**m.s. Redcherries**, author of *Mother*

Cicatrizing the Daughters

FLOWERSONG
PRESS

poetry by

SAMANTHA MOE

FLOWERSONG
PRESS

He had developed a superstitious fear of the instant, that tiny hole through which all the time available to human beings must pass.

—César Aira, *Varamo*

table of contents

Cicatrizing the Daughters

Para Esmeralda, Jorge, y Rosa,
con todo mi corazón.

Grief Birds

We know what you are, say the pale birds who won't leave my apartment. *Eldest daughter, you are no certain thing.* Telling me I inherited stove coils, a bad sense of humor, they have gaping mouths, curled fingers, flaws bundled in grandmother's fabric. Abuelita would never stand for this. I imagine she would unravel hundreds of feet of yarn, like buds and red flowers, ven aquí, she would say, dejame ver and together we'd rub ointment into the cracks in my skin. She is gone, I don't have a lighter, I use my phone to illuminate her soul-space, lay on her bed, open her drawers. I feel her heart draped over the apartment like a smooth July storm. I can't escape. I miss the man at the bodega who knows my order by heart, want to stuff sandwiches in my bra, can't eat in front of mother, who no longer wants meat in the house. *What about the chickens you loved?* I ask her. She shrugs. They were only interesting for their heads, she says, kisses my head, tells me I smell like pesuña, but now I am older, I can't remember if she meant horse hoof or melon, foot or beak or lo siento. When I ask my mother if she will ever abandon the upper West side, she laughs so loud on the phone my ears ring. I miss the loud nights, the oil, coco helado on the corner of Amsterdam and Broadway. The red birds are still here. They are hearts, they are grief, reminding me of how I long for a crowded apartment space. Once my uncle came from Puerto Rico, and I was so nervous I lost half my Spanish, I tried to tell him about the drunk couple leering at me on the 1 train, how they found out I was a writer and told me about the time they went to see Jacques Derrida give a talk right before he died. He said, *the act of opening a book was like the moment an angel stopped the kill.* When I try to tell this story, I forget the word for wings, I forget the angel's name. I wave my hands around and my family ignores me. This isn't about him or him or him, it's about [pero, cállate, it's not time yet to admit your identity, no static thing, could get you thrown out of the home, remember, she told you not to tell the rest of the family.] Well, es que no me siento bien, decaying on the dining room rug, the birds are not my sisters but my exes, I can see hatred and scorn in their eyes. Mí corazón, you would be different, I know you wouldn't ring the bell, we can't alert the grandmothers. Once we were gathered in the dining room after abuelito's funeral, sharing food. My cousin asked why everyone was upset and I told him gently that Jorge had passed away. He replied, *what are you talking about? He's under the table.* [I would bring you home with me, if I didn't have to hide—but I'd have to hide.] You'd know to step on the molding in the hall, you'd lift my head in the faded kitchen light and ask me where it hurts. I thought I'd be able to quell the ache when you approach but así es, a vulnerable and open wish that is me longing to be a feathered thing, some might call me magnificent, you could take me home or you could just take me around on your shoulder. This could be worth it, but I've been banned from telling you. How do I reach you. How do I get out of here. There are only ghosts left and the paint peels and I can run, but only so far.

antes

I want to know if you are proud
of me. Instead, I ask about mourning
doves, street pigeons, the bear sleeping
soundly in your backyard, curled like
a bug in the patch of red flowers, I want
to know if you still harbor red cement
spiders whose names I forget, do you
remember when we peeled maduros
with our fingers, I could only eat sweet
and salty, every meal was platanos
and turkey, yellow rice with peas
picked out, deep bowls of chicken
noodle soup, potato wedges, clear
onion and celery, I should have eaten
all the vegetables, I should have
remembered your middle name. I'll
be back soon, late in the evening on
the 1 train, and even though I know
New York City has turned itself
inside-out again, I never understood
how to say goodbye. The heat is off
in the winter, the doors have fifteen
coats of paint, they can only be
opened if I smack my hip into their
centers, doors making terrible sounds,
doors hiding bundles of fabrics you
haven't used since your fingers

stopped working, gauze and glitter
I wrapped around my shoulders
waiting for you to heat up breakfast
bread and butter, the only space I
haven't relapsed in is Manhattan.
Definitely in the Bronx. Yes Riverdale,
Boston, South Carolina, Illinois, now
Alabama. I don't want to talk about it.
I need attention at your dinner table. I
don't think I can see the ghosts on my
own. When I return, will I have dreams
about hidden city doorways, alternate
realities beneath the cement? Or will I
be so focused on whether I can survive,
capture your essence from a photograph,
recover the real pearls, the thick coats
hanging in abuelita's room, I'm afraid
of the clawfoot tub, my reflection in the
golden bell, tired and hiding food, drinking
the evening in, will I be too concerned
with staying alive to communicate with
you? if my mother and I don't fight, I
won't go to the bookstore where I suffer
through heartbreak. If I don't get lost, I'll
go to the ornament parade downtown. Rest
in the glow of the Christmas tents, I'll return
when you're having dinner prayers, let's
kneel in front of your statues, you'll be
rubbing a Mary figurine between warm
palms, I think I'll have a second rosary,
a woman I was once deeply in love with
pulled the string off my neck and the pale
pink beads scattered like stars. Do you

know what I mean? Do you know you're the only one left who loves me, or have you forgotten that, too?

La Amapola

Those days my name became torn, things were similar to hurt, what was the point of anything, still wondering, but god, the amber fields were paradise, before someone grabbed the jaw you might have asked why, it still matters, would things be better with more or less roses, wanted love by the bonfire but quickly my feelings were stolen, please don't blame me, what was once nirvana is now a straight razor, please float into the sky with goggles on, I'm dreaming of the garden again, wishing someone fought for me back then, if I'm not wearing red on the outside then what am I doing, can't name feelings, this could be paradise, this could be a sea of desert, silvery-green and neon, did you see forktail beneath the surface, mourn your wings, wish I had leather bags of money and crimson in my hands, nothing matters in all that ocean, in dreams you are swimming at midnight and I'm twilight, red algae kelp, sick coral and a shallow heart, I remember thinking there had to be more so I plucked myself out of the narrative and now I live as a little skin slice, please wash your face, don't forget about me, don't hit your head on the flip, red string seaweed in the surf, abandonment, time.

This isn't another story of how we counted money in Hell, but it could be

Raspberries in bowls, you left rhubarb for crusted copper roads, buildings inch together, windows are knives, you hid your city somewhere—will you know how to return after all this fight? Will you sell back the rings, unstitch your name from every band, prick your fingers on keys and leaf points which hang false in the blown glass shop, your exes lurk in doorways and the fly amanita expresses its hunger, lines, edges of the street like code, the rugs are bags full of cut candles, the cinnamon store doesn't want you near, the ox tongue is waiting for your touch, this isn't a story of stealing or stealth but it could be a reclamation of love, an unstamping of faces from coins, but please put slender envelopes in their final resting spots, blow Charon a kiss before crossing the river, your beloved has left town but you'd never know, her earrings dangle like fruits from trees, thought you caught a strand of her hair against clay and brick, an awning made of slick stinkhorn and starfish, there is basket, there is chorus, there is octopus and squid, a crab reaching out at all angles, beautiful poison lesson land, where did you decide to abandon the coral, the wings, plastic covering fire flowers, the outline of her heart as it beats in the machine shop, her leftover bite on the back of your neck, no one cares about the vampiric drama or the dame selling scarlet, wax caps grow and you're almost out of diamonds, and what are we going to do about dinner? This isn't a story about hands, not about chords or ether, the empty cigarette pack you found laced with gems, your tobacco stained jars and the day the lakes crawled back into the sea, you knew you'd never return home again, time-time became the wire fire in the back of a station wagon, the extra jaws you grew just to enter into Hell, and the gasoline lobsters made you lonely, it's not like everyone has a sequined soul, it's not like you're sorry but you're starving, so into the house we go, I'm trailing behind with the hooks, I'm your protection but these days you call me a carnivorous bird, you take backs and shoulder blades into hands and I take badges, bandages, brooches and bricolage, stuffing oil paintings and sapphire peach cores into purses, I hope you understand.

Apartment Problems

she is trying to sell the original
bones of the house, romanticizing
the mold and the scallop-shelled
hallway, which is no static space, I
walk into dreams between the living
room and the kitchen, the dining
room table is honey, did you forget
to push the ac-unit out great
grandmother's window again, did
you remember to seal the drawers
from the burglars and the pigeons,
you weren't here when we picked
apart turkey, spreading maduro over
its surface with our fingers, I used to
ask you to eat with me but you refused
and then you disappeared. I want to
tear down the blankets and knock gold
shells off the walls. you never cared
for the bamboo pot, I found orange
jars under your bed, have you been
sneaking tangerines to the neighbor
again? I am no stranger to loss or non-
love, it's my fault I thought you'd stay
but we work better on opposite sides
of the city, you like stretch and I prefer
blush, I thought you loved me because

you asked on my Oasis records, you
let a magician in the front door, but you
take and you mistake me for family.

Eldest Daughter

I.

You arrive close to ten in the evening, dropped off by a train from
a car from a car, missing your scarf, father didn't feed you and his
new daughter's dog has eaten your toothbrush but still, you are
in Manhattan during winter, during an ornament festival, among
sparkling sculptures and warm yellow tents, shop keepers urge you to
purchase twenty-two-dollar star balloons, and why compromise? No
one listens when your hands are empty.

II.

Half-asleep on the train, your mind splits between sewer rats and the
sea, for would it not be raw December magic if all that dark subway
space were filled with king crabs and grey squid, those fish with hidden
teeth luring you into the subway-grates-turned-sand, tunnel-turned-
trench, the conductor is an eel. Emerging on Broadway, you are no
longer underwater, just hungry with only enough cash for a croissant
that you wind up giving away. This will not be the last time you are in
Manhattan; you must make a promise to yourself to return when not
lost, recover your mother's paintings, pocket your great grandmother's
prayer beads and knit flowers, don't let she who never loved you stop
you.

III.

But you're upset anyway, scorned by the freedom of non-leaking
rooftops, wishing your building had a green awning over the stained

stoop, someone to know your name and open the door, stairs without holes, the doorbell can stay but the unlocked rooms must be emptied. Hate her teeth, hate her hands, hate her red nails and the way she rests against the gilded hallway mirror, why does she get to shrug at the entrance, why does she know the bodega cats by name, does she not remember late night talks and deli sandwiches stuffed in bras for warmth, the hot chocolate you had near Columbia, a filthy ledge overlooking Central Park, the hippo statues, the green noodles, the love, the Vix, the mothers. Eventually you are no one to her, nothing more than another stranger in the dollar store, she doesn't know how you longed to continue a decades-long tradition of being the family member who read their daughter's diaries, mother's cursive in French and Spanish, grandmother's letters, cousin's journals stuffed with secret money.

IV.

And what of it, Broadway, you want to take every pretzel-eating pigeon home, you want book releases the day of, you want pink elephant statues and the 99-cent store cat, you want what you want, you miss the New York of youth, it is no certain thing, you are in your father's house, cross-legged on the kitchen floor taking pictures of bowls of onions, tomatoes your stepmother grew, deep jars of green leaves, he laughs when you say someday you might want a yard. Does the floor remember your phone calls, your crying, do the walls recognize you are still an addicted spectacle, driving dozens of hours across the country for anyone who claims to care about your heart, and what a shock, this time he cooked a roast for you, there is even avocado fanned out like a green wing, there are seasoned mushrooms that are not the vegetables of your dreams but they will do, there is a three-month-late birthday cake, buttercream frosting, at breakfast you beg to be fed more than once. The espresso makes you sick but you drink it anyway, sift through the kitchen at two-am to look for something to take, finding instead used spoons and cereal bars in a half-sealed dollhouse, no one gives you toothpaste, no one checks when you, eldest daughter, are sick in the night, presented with two options for sleeping, either a haunted cloth-covered couch in the music room or a couch that is made of twisted lawn chair plastic painted blue.

V.

When at last you arrive at your destination you must clean the house. Hide your identity in tinfoil, hide turkey subs in your coat, take photos of the mist-filled lawn as if to say, yes you returned, but at what cost, but you're still alive, but are you still, but are you listening, but are you certain you will protect yourself this time.

Windy Blue Nights

Your father's dinner table spread includes a red candle in the center, melted just enough so it looks like a caved-in tomato, or maybe the caved-in heart of a blue whale, you don't recognize shapes, you're uncertain. Your stepmother cradles a puppy's head like a baby, your sister is next to you and trying not to cry. No one speaks to you for over half an hour. The house smells of spices and red wine. Your body knows the score, knows how to make your heart into a diamond pin so as not to alert the others that you are still something to be yelled at, not someone.

And the kitchen floor is warm, there are identical sets of espresso mugs, stirring spoons, mason jars whose linings are soaked with olive oil, each stuffed with leaves from his garden, you start to wonder if the plants keep track of the yelling, do the trees remember who did the planting, because if your sister dragged dirt into the house he would have yelled at her, if he wasn't happy with his knees he would have blamed your stepmother, but look at how green the leaves are, he says someday if you get your own yard you can grow something, too.

Correction: he says *if* you get your own lawn.

At night you walk around the first floor—you're not allowed on the second—looking for something to take with you. An item to remember the house, because your father says they'll be moving but he doesn't know where yet, and likely won't tell you when the time comes. They'll disappear from your life, just like others before them, just like your other family members who never wanted anything to do with you. But you're alone in the night, and your scars are now healed, or whatever that means because they're not going away.

Don't you remember deep blue nights spent sobbing on this floor? You carved a way out for yourself, so why do you still feel stuck.

It feels good to drive away.

You leave at dawn for the ocean house, house closest too salt and brine, house of a thousand burnt secrets, wrapped secrets, secrets tucked beneath leaves, twisted in branches free of berries, your ex's cigarettes still damp in the faded sun. Ocean house has many nicknames, but you can't talk about that right now. It's not time, yet, to peel away the layers of hurt, to reverse the dissociation—if such a thing is even possible.

Healing is leaving, healing is never, healing is always, healing is the quiet pocket of night when, windows down, you are driving around in the New England cold, yes you are crying but you left your tools at home, you're tossing words into woods, you're hoping to reach someone someday, maybe in the middle of the night, maybe not, too reach each other with green hands and flowers for lungs, we're not going to yell at each other, you can lay down your armor, but keep it within arm's length, healing is healing is time is absurd, is tired, is late, is waiting, maybe, waiting.

Ocean House Sestina

ocean house stands as tall as button mushrooms in the night
but when the moon makes her appearance so too does the house
unfurl into toadstool steps, blue curtains, stained glassware
that spells out a name I thought I'd forgotten. it's unfair
to claim we've run out of time when time was not real from
the start. when you arrive, you perch on the windowsill,

coat pockets full of oyster mushrooms and enokis, the sill
looks big enough that I might sit too, but I don't want night
to catch us together, I'm afraid you'll leave if I say. from
the deepest chamber of my clamshell clamped heart, house
full of beech clusters, I whisper to the swamp what is unfair
meaning I am afraid of the truth that does not greet me gloss

of the floor is slick, I edge towards your presence, you're glass
of rosé in hand, you're floral skirts fanned out like suns, still
I feel a rush when you ask me if we can go to the kitchen. fair
food is stuffed into all the cabinets, funnel cakes dusted with night
time sugar, deep-fried BLT's there are green cookies and House
hides well the cotton candy tubs but we find them, sea foam

and echo of light opal, each cluster tastes savory. from
fried ice cream clusters in the stove to homemade jelly, glass
panes made of sugar that resemble playing cards, I crave house
wrapped bacon-corn, please feed me blue ribbons, still
my shaking hands which seem to only write the past. night
is a caramel pear covered in drizzle and sea salt, it's fair

to hide bundles of money in the silverware drawers. love, flair
of your stories always draws me close, please tell me from
where do I find the courage to ask you to stay here. midnight
iced tea is navy with sugar, royal blue with coffee cream, glass
is not proper for this occasion, let's drink from our hands, will
you take me into the chest so I may confess, I need your hard house

press to my oven-nicked hands, I've stopped longing for houses
to save me, it's the relationship between refrigerators, unfair
yet perfect sycamore trees, it's the stairs inside and out, *still*
I think this house is going to save me but only if you stay. from
the kitchen table I see a circus tent unfold in the living room, glass
eyed contortionists and tightrope walkers call your name, night

isn't nearly as good as when you're gone, yet you leave my house
for this inner-space, red tent cloth and buckets of fried foam,

I hear you singing as the tent extinguishes itself, don't tell you
it's unfair I love you because it's my fault for believing glossy-

toned springtime lies you tucked into berries. the tent folds
itself into a pocket square. I climb the nearest windowsill and
disappear into another night.

And in July I am losing track of myself near a tide pool

I see your reflection in the shallow end of the tide
pool. It's another greasy July day and I am already
sick of myself. We crouch on sun-hot rocks whose slick
surfaces our mothers have warned us from, flip-flops
in one hand, an old bucket in the other, I wait to capture

the crab. But she doesn't want to reveal herself, and I am
distracted by iridescent mica, a stone my father used to tell
me was worthless. I remember once when I was even younger
he gave me a crate full of amethysts to keep, later swapping
with me for a fossilized fish, as if to say, *if you stay right here*

you too will be beautiful. But I am sliding on new hot rocks
careful not to get too close to you. We don't love each other
anymore, but I still love you, the difference being there is no longer
a love collective, no longer an us, no more phone calls, we won't
sing nicknames into shells, but I know I'd call the lobster *Bunny*

you can be *Ray of Sunlight on Silt*, or *Mint Shells Hiding Deep*
maybe *The Brine* and *The Banana Popsicle Stick Burning a Hole in my
Pocket.* I want to give the joke to you, but you call me a Sagittarius
before walking into the sea. And I am still here, and anyways, what's
the point in leaving when people sometimes change, maybe you come
back and we do everything right, this time when I call you answer

I won't admit I care too much; I'll go to the beach by myself, wouldn't it be fun to love the perfect me, the me who isn't reaching a hand down below and grabbing, frantically, at any crab. The new me is quiet, maybe even be asleep on this rock, hair spilling over the edge, the crustaceans give me a trim and you'd walk over, say how you got it all wrong, you'd be like *oh, I love how casual you are with your neck on the ledge*, and my heart wouldn't even be in my throat, my hands wouldn't scratch at my sides

I could say, *I forgot you loved bunnies,* and you'd be hurt yet intrigued that I named this crab for you, can I name other things, too?

Yes, the new me might say. She'd rise, half asleep and hungry, slide aviators down her nose, and say, *look, you see that?* And we would look at the sand dunes. *That is a dove.* She'd point to the ocean foam. *That is a checkers game.* She'd nod at the sun. *That is a clover.* She'd point to her heart. *And that is an empty pail.*

What color? You might ask, thrilled by the lack. *Hmm,* she'd say, because it would have to be the opposite of your favorite color. *Green,* she'd say. And we would laugh and laugh before new fathers arrived, loving fathers, fathers who knew our middle names and fathers who didn't yell, a field full of fathers to take us home,

and we'd fall asleep in the back seat of a grey minivan, warm and coated in sand, maybe we'd be holding hands, maybe we'd go back to your house, and one hundred fathers would cook us one hundred dinners. Everyone would get our names right. Everyone would stay, and the new me would rest easy, knowing I'd never have to say *love* again and mean it. The new me out there, somewhere, even now without scars, without grape blunt wrappers and crush letters.

I think she might be twirling a lettuce leaf around like a parasol, I think she hears you, *my darling*, you are saying over and over again, and we start crying from laughing so hard.

Pepper Bells

We stand in the kitchen, eating bell peppers by hand and joking
about how sweet the moon hangs, a pale tangerine just above
the restaurant across the street. And you're here again, after you
said you wouldn't return to messy grass patches, lost your grey
heart in a cabin, called to the faded creature who once slept
in your Sala, maybe I should have known we would meet again,
after all, there were conejitos in my front yard again, it's like you
knew I would be near, heart barely hanging on after years of lies
and birds who abandoned me. But you don't want to hear about
loss, you want to hear me tell stories about bells then pajas turning
to pajaros, how peppers how can be emptied of seeds and replaced
with grandfather clock anchors and pendulums, how the green peppers
make music when they've been left out in a rainstorm, you're curious
about whether I've been sleeping, if I still leave the phone off
its cradle, is the entire house filled with sounds that could be dots
or could be echoes? And there is this persistent echo whenever
I'm around you. I eat a pepper. *Was it bad? It was real. Was it real?*
It was night. Was it cold? It was empty. You Are storing crushes in
hurricane jars, you want to know how to empty the bells, explain how
their seed columns are like heart valves, and you can scoop, scoop, scoop
out my accumulated feelings. Was it bad, you ask. It was nothing, I reply.
The others nod their heads, offer their hands to us. We forfeit the
pepper cores, I abandon my heart to you, watch as you take it to the
sink. For a wash, I ask. For a revisit, you say, flicking the switch to the
garbage disposal.

I wake up each week / just to head towards you

I'm not supposed to trust you. My hair is falling apart
and I've been staring at my reflection in your mirror
for ten minutes when your soft knock shocks the focus
I don't belong, yet you've invited me in and anyway
what's a good dinner without someone to waste
your time? Tonight, you wear a dozen flowers in your

braid and your eyeliner is smudged like mine. I can't bear
to hold your gaze so I act the part of a too-blue heart
and my flowers have molars, you reach out to encase
my dreams in your scent. I know this old talk, mirror-
and-jewel toned horse statues guard the kitchen, say
you'll defend me if they ever find out, say my focus

is shit, say you'll follow me into hell and then the opus
room where opals and acorns adorn the shelves, your
fear is that I'll leave, my fear is I'll be eaten alive by way
of whatever hungers are lurking, these days we part
late, we pretend to hate each other, we are lake shimmer
and we only eat gorgeous green-gold oysters from bed. Taste

the divine, string along friends, I'm not praying in haste,
I'm not lurking in the shawls of pasture reeds, moats
of cream-dream daffodils, there is eternal spite, mirror-
mirror mimosa dahlias, quilt-fire gladiolas, real lilies, you're
catching me looking your way but baby don't tear apart
my reputation, I don't want anyone else to hurt me. Away

in the garden I'm not waiting for kiss, for fight, for spry
leaves and ankle tears, oh someone to fold my heart, waste
my time, it helps the heat leave my ears and hands. this part
is always a sinew, whose side am I on anyway? For us
to be in the same space is just another Sunday night, you're
right, they won't suspect, but what if I want to light mirror

me on fire, what if I've burnt my life down before? Simmered
in the ashes of destruction and heartbreak, I had a way
with words but now I can't recall psalms—to tell your
truth or to lock your soul in an oak chest, well, a taste
of who I really am is as delicious as a sea-sugar, so focus
on me, we're in this together and no one will bear us apart,

we're mirror images of wasted time, we silver-cowboy boots
and diamond choker doves, we could put the matches away,

just once I'd like my way to not hurt my hands, I'd like you to
privately hold this star, show us that lying can win, that your

protected affection is not going to lose, I'm better at pretending;
let's return to the party, darling we can't let them catch us
without knives up our sleeves.

Lightning Yarn

We are surrounded by tall, thin trees whose leaves I don't recognize. I must drive half an hour to the supermarket to call my mother, and she knows something is off, says my words form a knife through the receiver, and all I have given her are half- formed stories whose empty spaces I'll have to fill in when I escape this place. I don't want to eat in front of the others, I want to lay on the roof and let the thunder and lightning tango my heart into growing cartoon wings, and my love will fly away into the night, and I'll survive without my mind turning silver and twisted as a screw. The storm clouds play piano, the evening does not care to remember my name, I aim to be consumed, I want to open the doors of your heart. Instead, I am in bed, I am waiting for your soft laugh in the hall, your fingers on the door handle, maybe we'll talk about our mothers, our siblings, our desires for the earth to form blankets, no more consume-me-whole, no more velvet green dreamland, we can eat flowers, we can make eggs and bacon and feed them to the roots. When at last you enter, I am no longer of breath, nor dirt, nor hands, nor books, I am absent mindedly eating toast with credenza berries, I am the weathervane and the dancers in the center of the house, I am giving up my love to you and you are taking it to ribbons, running away while I watch, and the storm gets worse but my dreams fill with tide pools, I think I see your reflection in the water but when I try to reach in, I see it's just me, and I am swallowed by sea urchins and ruby starfish, but also, I abandon bed, I am at the dinner table, quietly pushing around lime weeds with my fork.

Hull

I.
Heaven, would you inspect this tattoo on my hand, do I
still dwell inside your heart, what about our bond, and
the oyster boat, the way water curled around the hull, hadn't
slept and my eyes were glassy, the moon didn't care, I should
have brought heavier nets, core of the house stuffed in a lamp,
fish confetti, try and understand I was in a hurry towards you.

II.
And I found your love letter inside an apricot pit, I would
have followed you into deep grey water, where jealous starfish
hate your beauty, cry about your sea-urchin earrings, why did
you leave trout in my room, won't you find me for dinner, care
to imagine it's you who never stays, not me?

III.
Water in my wine glass, I'm daydreaming again, of light fixtures
and thick rugs. I miss the mold, and I would sleep under the desk
if you'd let me back.

IV.
And I know I know, you think longing is a trap, your sand-colored
hair shimmers when you laugh, I doubt you remember what I like
to eat for dinner, why I hate the claws on the tub, bet you've got
snares for ghosts, you're too golden to be haunted. softer this time,
you want marshmallow honey after dinner, no more crying, let's
find our ways back and if you let me return, I promise I'll surrender

my buttered lungs and too-blue pigeon hearts, about those jaws you
left in the sink—

VI.

I'm an herb now, core of my body is a pad of parsley, screw human,
share your pots with me, deep-bellied spatulas, please water the weeds,
impress the mulch with your statues, will you whistle in the storms, toss
away letters, about that apricot, I don't need you to follow me but try to
understand I'm bored without you, I am the how and the weathervane,
the good voice, water and whatever, how about we forgive the lack of
mermaids, we can resurrect sunken ships, I'll gloss my lips, I remember
you always liked folding laundry in the waves.

Green Suns

I.

I dig small green suns out of the earth, patting the dirt after
to say, *thank you*, or maybe I meant to say goodbye to anyone
who might still seek after I run home. It's been raw storms,
the air smelling of persimmons and sweet cantaloupe,

everything overripe and only a little damp. I know blue
heart had replaced my red, then blue bones, everything a lake
inside my body that I need to come to terms with, yet lake
as a synonym for lost love is insufficient.

The hurt of the green suns in my hands, their small flames
yoked, glue of the surrounding ferns drips below feet, kept
my goodbye sealed in a layer of the earth, moss, algae blossoms
from old slopes near the valley of the acid lake.

II.

The thing is, it's been a raw storm day for two weeks and I
no longer understood raw feelings, did not know my purpose with
my mother, the lake tight as plastic wrap, its sediment too secretive,
coat of water buttoned down the middle only rippled on Tuesdays.

Shirt hems are the most seductive. I love collars, sighs,
pockets deep enough to hold a person. The true truth hurts
more than the lie truth. I have been betrayed.

III.

Goodbye to her tender heals, I will miss my own hands, the lake
calls out to me to *just leave*, and yet I stay. Smooth dirtturned to
coils from limey worms, scabbed beetles, those hope
ants coated in raw sugar blooms, everything alive, tucked
inside ignored her hands.

The blue day continues to unfold across the sky, thick struck
clouds hurt one another over hurting treetops, I ignore electric owls,
raw grey ghost turtles crawling from holes of sycamores, a snake
wrapped around my ankle, I begin to sing to her.

IV.

Shy of my mother picking up the other line, I shake loose centipedes,
cry, clamp a hand over my mouth at the familiar *hello*. Lobe of
Heaven's and earring pressed to dirt phone, probably ate a feast
of white chocolate croissants with her lover that day, blue silk
bathrobe parted at the breasts, *is this a prank call?*

Her raw voice, stained from weed and breakfast and maybe love,
the hurt I felt when I let the sweet-toed bugs fall gently back to earth,
goodbye to a slammed call farewell, my blue heart at the very least
responding with an *I hate hope, you fed me raw orange slices in my sleep,*
I starved for your love and now I'm locked out of a lake that doesn't even
belong to you, how dare you, Heaven, hello? Dirt falls in bursts.

sea/salt/sugar/phones

cool spaces of the back rooms, dull blue refrigerator
doors, it's June and the restaurant's main phone rings
at all hours. there are crates of oranges, a hazy citrus
dessert coated in cobweb sugar; knives thin enough
to peel apples, knives for oysters, knives for lobsters
and bowls of sculpted butter in the shape of clams,
hearts, hands holding pearls like rosary beads.

I wonder if Abuelita's rosary still hides in the back
room of the house. She used to keep powdered
sugar in Ziploc bags, she made *coco helado* in early
summer, milkshakes in the evening, she would have
handled the dinner rush with ease. time is a root
around my heart, I come home smelling like vegetable
oil and soda bubbles, I crave coffee cake and *huevos
mollos* whose crepe-paper encasements I once
discarded all over the floor of someone else's wedding.

Por fin, my heart thrums once more at a steady beat,
I am still having dreams about my family but at least
I'll be home again, to see the seed of the moon appear
over the lake, to walk the gum-streaked streets of
Manhattan in late, jewel-toned July, I will leave
the restaurant and toss the ashes of my past into
the sea.

I must stop myself from running into the kitchen
to ask if I can lick the spoon. I must return to the
gods and the grills, the girls who've been waiting
tables for millennia, the green aprons and not-yet
ripe pears from the grocery store on 110 and Broadway,
I promise I'll check all the drawers; I'll take your
memories home with me. come back to haunt me,
I could use an extra hand. we can press our hearts
between wax paper and hide them in the bottom
of your favorite gloss-toned blueberry pies. I'll be
safe this time, but please call me in the morning,
just in case.

Manhattan, again

and to think that I would forgive you
collapsed clocks, your grandmother's petal
necklace, hiding sandwiches in our bras,
you made me break up with New York City,
you ruined sun and stoops I can't eat in
front of my family but at least I know how
to eat pizza while crossing the street, did
you forget about the hot pink parrots in queens,
how we fought to survive after coming out,
the thick grass in patches of Central Park, the
man with the bubbles, how I got lost in evening,
I want to smudge you out of pictures, I want to
rest in my mother's bedroom and I want to
take the sewing machine back, smack pigeons
off the sill with a fan, I want to collapse the
apartment until I can see every room and I know
inherently that though the building has kept
the score I now can tell if I am alone or watched
I'll sleep on the rugs in our dead relative's
rooms, I'll be the one to save this space from
itself, from the rats, from your missteps and
crowded cabinets. When she finally dies, please
leave her for me. Make sure her ghost has room,
to observe my cooking skills and my cleanly
sliced platano disks, I'm asking you to leave
the living room light on, leave your name at
the door, leave and don't return, and to think

we could ever love each other again, not after
breakfast, not without our mothers, not
in the prayer room, not on the rosary, not on
my life, not even though you hugged me when
I came back and I caught you grimacing in the
gold mirrors.

During which the witches descend into the haunted house together

If you're fine with the decay, we can be remarkable. I tell you
about the architecture which consumes my mind, and you think
I'm so smooth, how could a house follow someone so far out into
fields where abandoned wells stand, dotting the landscape with dry

patches of grass, the occasional circling of small purple flowers I
used to pluck and tie together in wreaths for my grandfather's
head, but what about the way the porches wrap and snap until
they connect in one looping square, and their surfaces are coated

in all the toads and frogs from the swamp down the street, the bog
in the backyard, did you know I'm keeping my heart safe for you
if you don't mind the hauntings then we can head out together
traverse the floors of the ancient and many-floored house with its

beautiful rouge carpets, the mermaids stamped into the foyer, the way
the kitchen has a habit of growing waxy plastic leaves in coils and its
shadow, a second smaller kitchen, is covered in boughs of ivy and empty
pots and pans, beneath lives twisting floors like too-soft bricks, no one

knows where to put their cigarette ashes, I want you to take the glasses
gently from my face and know their designated spot on the nightstand
my heart wants, ragged with haunt, and while you're at it could you watch
my back as we descend, I think if I reached for your hand I would twist

turn to ash in an instant. And inside these walls which contain the history of the house itself a thousand endless movements crushed in liminal spaces where ghost lobsters and demon crabs glow unnatural shades of amber and azure there is a pasture of velvet, there is a ladder, we ascend

between thin layers of kitchens, stacked as one boiling cake on top of another and I'm desperate to make it out of the maze alive—with you by my side—and if you don't mind the way I scratch at my chest when I can't breathe, if you, too, cover all the surfaces during a storm, if you house

ruined horses, if you have soft stars in jars atop your highest cabinets, and might you also have a beehive with a pool of honey where the bugs can swim, and did you know there is another four-letter word for love but it hasn't been revealed yet, but would you guess I have something

else written on my tongue for you, and could you put away your teeth to listen, but would you take care to not insult the ghosts who have never left this place, so I guess we arrive together, intertwined like strands or rope or hands, we could make it through, you and I, and if we live to see oceans together, would you know to lead me along where it hurts? Would you trust the best shells are a little further out, leave your broken shards in the expertly labeled foyer drawers, then maybe we can make it through just fine, maybe we'll drive like darling flames to lick the salt into soup bowls

and stationary holders, well did you know there is a demon holding the core of this home and every time she hears me laugh she shakes, it only serves to bump us closer together, my teeth accidentally brushing your earlobe, I'm going to break your heart, I'm going to stoke your crush into a bonfire.

my family doesn't know I'm queer /
at least the ocean does

We break up somewhere off the Atlantic and I won't hand you the anchor, I won't help with the wine glasses and the guests, if you need me, I'll be in my cabin (you don't ((need me)) and I know this, telling myself I should have done better, and what was I expecting, you touched my arm, I haven't been numb since. My father would have warned me not to love a woman like you—if he even knew his daughter was queer, if he even knew she was lost at sea and stubborn as the waiting jaws of a lantern fish, if he were here, he might agree—your eyes look like the lights in the woods ashore, those same woods you and I carried crates of crustaceans to cook, the wedding wasn't for another few hours, we saw the brides chasing each other through woods like deer, their hair black and honey-hued, *That could be us*, I recall you saying. I looked over only to find you were focused on rollups in deep green cloth, you were rotating the plates so *indispensable, hot, overwrought,* and *respectfully* were facing the guests, I won't repeat the poem because I know it is your favorite, I saw the refrain tattooed on a woman at the library, you were trying to tell me it didn't mean anything, I know better. Service is storm themed, I don't care, I'm downstairs praying for hail to create separation between us, you might try to say sorry again, I won't be able to hear you over the cacophony of blue, grey, crystal, I toss the anchor overboard, an apology I found carved into its rusted base (why shouldn't the sand dollars tear, or the starfish weep from frustration?) There are so many anchors, many half-eaten ships, our history is hopeless, hips, harmony turned into fists, I don't trust you near my lips. The dinner guests are laughing, leaning back in their navy-blue booths, each printed with cartoon crabs, whales, and seals, I don't have the energy to tell them. Real aquatic creatures have scars, oils, bleached coral bruises, their beloved captain once threw trash into the sea, she tried to out me to my mother, she told me it was liberating to turn off her mind for a few minutes at a time. Feel like I'm becoming a barnacle on the ship, when I uncork wine all that comes out are small sturgeons, vaquita ghosts, a moray eel tangling around my wrist like a bracelet There are seagrasses and diatoms blue as the promise you gave before biting off my throat. Hundreds of fins rise from the sea, there is a mermaid calling my name, she says sea lettuce is better than iceberg lettuce, I guess I believe her, why would someone with scales lie to me, me, me? So we leave, everything is waterwheel and eel grass, a parrot feather in bottles, messages in coralline, there is the locket you once gave me (now old) floating away towards gorgeous glittering water hawks, I'll later hear the stories about how you were (*so*) heartbroken you let your house turn into a forest but I won't care, I'll be older in a cable knit sweater, I'll be frequenting the water bars with my demigod girlfriend, the bartenders will say *Oh, she sure loves to swim*, I'll say *That she does*, before we skip out on our tab to head out into the icebox heart of night. I won't mind I'm cold all the time, my heart has turned blue (I'm with a new-you), she'll say I'm beautiful, blue as lobster pearls and clam paws, now we're no longer playing games, we're haunting in the tide and the wide-open bite of a waxen, ex-shaped jellyfish scar around your ankle. Are you icing the raw away? Or are you giving into the shore, the hurt, the razor fins of clear-eyed manta ray gazes, I'll never reach for you again, I'd rather give up my heart then my hands, you'll be alright, please take back the past, please tell me you're done with all that, but please don't forget to tell me you're still alive.

There are parties in the second layer of hell, but I don't go anymore

Hades doesn't want anyone to know it's her birthday. She loves
blush and salmon, ballet slippers and naps beneath dogwood
trees. She has a throne hiding in her house made of construction
paper and her middle name is *Hickory*. Late Thursday I head out
to ivy pastures where toads with hot pink hearts heal before summer,
the air smells vaguely of lava and coal. I remember shutters
whose surfaces were embossed with roses; French bread coated
in jam, I draw ashtrays from the garden pools, I stick a lid
of taffy beneath a stone but it's likely dissolving, what with
the fire and all. If I were magic, this wouldn't be happening.
I would be sweet-tempered with creamy-orange hair and
decaying flame heart. There would be punch and prayer and
parties, love tasting like bubblegum, sleepy days eating cooled
berry pies. It's not a rage thing. I mistake your boxelders for oaks,
I say I hate the spruce. Forget the elm. If I could sing lullabies
like a fawn harp, I would. Know I'd twist myself into the surface
of the moon so you might have something to look at each
night, know I'd enter bearing sunsets in my arms, we could
be exhausted from hours spent late on the kitchen floor.
There are crepe paper clouds in your house. When I arrive,
everyone is gathered around the stove, commenting on how your
wallpaper smells like vanilla scones and Saturdays. I don't
let myself dream the whole weekend, keep track of your moods
in a notebook, draw an image of your face in the margins. Do you
still count the nights you feel haunted, do you still save your memories
in jars? Maybe you'll cast frosty spells for hours. Maybe you're in love

despite the bitter curtains of time, between clock shatter, hand pierce, pendulum erosion. It's never *I might love someone else even though I'm a Libra*, it's always, *I am unlovable, and winter is in my head for a thousand days*. It's effort, however teal, numbing tiles onto the bathroom floor. It's how much I miss the Underworld, your guard dogs, the messenger birds and the basalt rock coasters. Moss and lichens, soil and starting points, I'll uncoil the forests and sift through the oceans, cast out my name, a dead sea star, to decay on your desk.

Fire

We light a fire in the middle of the night, after your parents
have gone to bed. The house shrouds the lawn in swaths
of chandelier light that I jump over, the backyard is hilly,
full of poisonous mushrooms and humans with clear eyes,
this forest is thick with fallen logs and wires twisted into
sculptures. We hardly leave the house, we're having pineapple
juice and conversations, we go running into the neighbor's
field. Our friend tells us stories of magnificent fires, hides
lettuce in his inner jacket pocket, there is summer rain and
a field of new mud, I pretend I'm not in love. I have dreams
of vegetables, the way you tuck your hair behind your ear,
pockets of quiets, bunny races, do the evening trees see my face?
I begin to wonder if my heart is echoing, affecting electricity,
am I the reason for my own disenchantment, still I keep on
coming to your house, running my fingers across old canvas,
oils make ridges which turn into waves, I want to fold myself
in half, I want to hide in your house, just like this, a ghost in
the clock in the hall, you won't be able to toss me away, you
won't be able to see my love from behind the numbers and
the hand twists.

To Fortify the Ingredients

1 tbsp	don't want to tell you how I feel
50g	I just want to talk about the eels
4	organ pipes
2	rustling thrombus
1/3 cup	coral larva
4	secret lava
1 tbsp	the fingers
¼ cup	red plate
5 tbsp	sea whip
18 ml	mushroom
2	oyster
Oven-baked	curl
¼ cup	toad stool
4/5 cup	hedgehog
1	milk
50g	the truffle of my heart
6	the table of contents protecting me from crying

Step 1

how come you get to see the otters, does anyone know how to tell the truth, my confession is a loose blown bottle cap on a brave blue turtle, maybe someday I'll be able to tell you but for now I'm aching with the unspoken, I'm giving secrets to sea urchins, I will try to remember your shape.

Step 2

I will write you poems about an ocean in the gymnasium and how the students all laughed when they saw the fish, and they cried at the whale, and anemone were red, and everyone had their hearts.

Step 3

I don't want to write about the collage, how personal it was to me, how personal it still is. This is more than I can handle, I only remember your faded shape because I'm incapable of letting go, I want to know if you remember how I lay on my stomach as we glued magazine cutouts to notebook pages, you at your desk, a thousand miles away, telling me it felt like we were in the same room. I don't remember if I still love you, or if I'm afraid of the feeling of loss, do you want to go back to the pit of the sea? We can stand at the edges and point, laugh as seals morph bubbles, contemplate how long we can sustain the coral, its hue is red, its hue is green, somewhere I see amber and cruise-surf frills, honey bun coils, I am leftover, I am not able to remember you because all I see is grief.

Step 4

you're off somewhere, fully alive and divine, I want this to reach you, I want the truth to break down your walls in the middle of the night, I want to know if you remember sneaking into my room real late, I made the mistake of telling you to come back again, because what do I know? Well, I know now not to ask for extra love, it's only going to push you away, can't ask for any adoration, can't have choice, can't have books, no songs, nor hands, that don't remind me of you.

Step 5

I am gone of strength, tired of the mind, unsure of devotion, this is not the worst, I want to keep hiding from you, look away,

5	lanterns
2	chocolates shaped like hearts
75	cartons of eggs in the noon-goo sun
18	the world 'vulnerable'
3	the shape of two hands cutting through the air
½ cup	a tomato
1	tears
9	glittering shark ornaments
120g	butter in a pan
6	gazing
1	round table
0	red birds
50g confetti	
2	lost trees
2	gorge is gorgeous
13	jumping into the lake
5	I wasn't there
1	I should have pocketed the pebbles you touched and given them to the elk-horn,

did we make it?

Heart Seeds

if I had known you would leave me for honeysuckle
red bees, focaccia foam, the shocking clouded Sulphur
old gems, a heart full of pear seeds, a bag full of Sundays

I would have asked for two hugs, I would have saved
my sobbing for when you turned your back. I knew it
would hurt to cry into the live-lime-greens

wheats, auburn fields, trills of birds sing a sorry for me. I
get lost on the walk home, you never accompanied me,
there is a stray cat, a bunny, a TV discarded, half-shattered

I am afraid to be alone, I am always alone. I wait for night,
for lilac skies before summer storms and you take my words
from your halls, might you still think of me when you eat
blueberries?

when you dip your scones into a coffee mug, shaped like
someone else's heart, I could rest right there, below the handle,
a crumb of a person—not even a ghost—an easy love, for you

wouldn't see me most of the time. Baby, do you still make
promises, might you hate my foxes, could you write a sonnet
before bed, do you still say love you, do you know my name

do you want to say a proper farewell, I could tell the owl to find
you, she might swap my letter for a worm, I think you'd still
know it was me, helpless, with excellent taste

you might give me apple cores; you might tell the owl to take
it easy, and maybe where I'm going, I won't need my heart; yes,
I would like that.

Green Goddess

It's not about the mushrooms, the halos, pistachio
shoes and a porch reaching out to grab me with both
hands. It's not even about the confetti, cherry-colored
birds in your backyard trees and your cat hates me but
your house loves hearts, why don't I have a center?

These days I wake to rain in my living room, where sheets of
frogs are here forever, I've never felt safe, we no longer
have dreams to share, it's about hearts turned inside-out
it's about how you lied to me, told stories about never-
ending orchards, curled trees that are not fists, you
promised fever dreams, red dough pies, but I'm petty
and I'm gone, someone told me to call you back but these
days I can barely get out of bed, why would I love, lush
coffee makes my lungs jump, God help, it's me again on the
kitchen floor, I spill asparagus and free tomatoes under a
table, it's petit filet mignon I tear apart with my hands, rare
veins, petty laughter and regret, why did you choose the hurt?

Art in the evenings, I sob on the 1 train, lick the subway, we
could have seen the whales together but no, these lives you've
knotted! The unsafely of evening! Poetry! and marinara sauce,
I should have marked your kitchen, cleaved my alphabet into
a letter until it admits, finally, freed and without lies, that you
were my hand in burning heart in non-pearl shell, a light
Tuesday, I hate you, pistachio muffins don't work for breakfast,
please return ready and raw, in no particular order: my picture,

glove, grease from bacon, your partner's earrings, abandon me, me, me in a car in a tunnel, toss me into the sea, don't leave without at least explaining why I meant nothing, here I will burn most of my words away, you will tease the end but we both know it's a quiet human, earth worms experiencing a feast but I hate cherries, yet if you were to pry open my palm and tell me, pistachio hearted fool, to swallow the green and the pit, told me to roll receipts into joints, toss hearts into the gone, I'd yet forget what you did, I'd impress upon the trees to observe your petty feet, I'd eat from your hand. But today I'll never trust my soul again. It's about the ascent. It's about how I'll bite love on the mouth.

Goldfield

You arrive at the party last, reckless as
sunflower, you don't want the others to
know you traded lungs and then some to get
through the doors, everybody knows that
you're ridiculous, who else would look good
wearing that citrine dress, tourmalines in
your ears, you're into honey and her cooking,
you love excess and you came with the
appetite, you came with the pen, the desire
to cut throats, do you remember staying up
late in the Slumber Hall whisking eggs until
your wrists hurt, your eyeliner was smudged
but you didn't care, told your ex you had
forgotten something at the store and she
mumbled someone else's name in her sleep
so you left for the hotel, the chefs love when
you sit on the counters, calling you *bold* and
sunshine, skin the lemons for the dish, skip
the tablecloths, take your no-bakes into the
craft room, accept that the drinks you are
given aren't potions for transportation, you
can write yourself out of this life, fondant
fancies and bring the rum, darling don't let
lemon curd become more charming than
you, don't bring mother into this, she looked
so pissed at the pool, toying with water lilies
while yelling at the neighbor, you've left it all

behind, magic and lime, threw the marriage proposal in the trash, you pretend to be strong but you're tripping over your dress, you're wishing you had fangs, praying to the old gods to sharpen the butter knives and the only saint who listens is a desperate man carving letters into the silverware, he stares at you from the dining room and asks why you even bother, let's show everyone what you can do with a limoncello, God knows you can make a tasty margarita, you cry at night in your room and your ex never mailed your things, lost socks with wolves and winter orange whiskey recipes, she's sipping a mango float somewhere and cursing you by both names, this isn't about truth or love, this isn't even about whether or not the kitchen is full of monsters, no, this is about how you paid your dues, swept dupe receipts and washed floors, now you're sweetened like fruit, they let you slice the fish with your fingers, they hand you ramekins of slushie, everything sparkles and the chandelier looks so brilliant you dream daily about eating it, you save your own life and you save the crumbs from the overtakes, your coworkers and fellow servers are calling you an angel, sweet as cake mix cookies, they don't know how you imitate art, screw the mimic and the woman at the clinic who told on you to your mother, and while you're at it, take, in no particular order: their hearts, pants, pears and satin handkerchiefs, a drink called *smash*, her high heels you loved so much, discarded matches and soy milk, those kisses that make your lips bleed, apple juice, and any knives you can get your hands on.

late Tuesday

surprise, I'm going to tell you about the heartache. I'll cook you grilled cheese beneath the burning orange lamps, I'm going to sigh when I cut the exquisite tomato. I think you think I'm not good (enough) and maybe you're right. or perhaps that's a fabrication and you, laying soft on the couch of velvet pillows, eyes open, cat on your chest, well maybe (maybe ((maybe))) open your judgment to the open air of Tuesday eve. I'll give you the benefit of all my doubt, I'll give to you carved potato halves with chives, old butter, can't promise honesty but what does that matter, so maybe your eyes are only open to gaze at the cat, so low and smooth is the night. I'm burning a piece of tender tomato, but it'll taste good, trust. (must we?) when I pry open the cabinet, a thousand rust-hued moths fly out. Maybe they could have been birds, if I'd loved more. I'm dusting off plates, I've dropped a mug, you stir. clamp my love back with a bite, someone stuff it in soup, make a guest consume the pump and blood, the hell. you take the plate with open arms. the cat sleeps on. love, who will care for me when I show what I've become? perhaps it's better this way, lonely. I'll let you keep the cat, open my closet and take too the heat, the water, all gloves. I'd rather persist on my own, determined and foolish, maybe still a little in love with you but what does it matter. maybe I'll miss you forever, did you ever think about that. of course, you don't mind, waxing on between bites about survival. I'll live through you just like I've lived through all the others. so now I'm alone, soaking in the tub, so what. when I open the soap vials, I conjure a man in the water warm as lamps on February porches. He will only last as long as the dampness in my hair takes to dry, takes me in his blue crush, maybe his heart is a half rubber sponge (and then some).

when the door clicks in the living room, I know you've left me, you and the cat, and my coat, my weed, my medication.

how late I'll let the house become chilly depends on sobbing, I'm dead in hands, glimpse the man made of soap who is, of course, also leaving. you'd do well to not to puddle in the bathroom. maybe to cultivate joy is to wrench open the mind. later, close to four, I find a tomato on top of a folded napkin. I open the note, shy to find out your last words. In rips and permanent marker ink that has bled into the counter I read: unkind.

NYC Moon In the kitchen at the party, eating sweet bread rolls and lobster valves, you have oyster juice dripping down your neck, you have gemstones and accusations at the ready, wondering if I'm writing lately, or maybe I'm giving into the exhaustion, am I stuck, do I still have your face. We're new bodies in grandmother's apartment, moist air and old spaghetti in the dishwasher, leaf calves on ceiling fans, back wraps, Vix, I switch my Spanish around in my mouth, I'm half sweet, mostly, I want to tell you stories that will make you love me again. And there's warm water and sand in the sink, a bar down the street where they know I'm queer, they let me hang my identity in the hall before heading home, *does she know you write about her?* They ask. *My mother? No, never*, nor does she know about the molded docks and green-grey slimes twisted around my feet, my ex was born in October, and she loves swimming as mourning, you now wave your hands around the room and tell me about dancing with the next-door neighbor, the affair you had with an older woman, and when it's my turn to speak all I can say is *barnacle blooms*, and *after*, and *she was my best friend*, the rule is no talk, no oyster ridges behind molars, no words, nor minutes, nor fewer, not fever, never finger, slower, scared, please, now, what, heart, stuffed, eels, and home is the curve of a weapon cleaving my identity in half, we all have a coming out story that involves our parents—mostly mothers—claiming non-forgiveness, claiming upset, claiming a blame on the cardboard house and the blue room full of inherited trauma, my mother used to keep nested horses in bags, foxes in drawers, ears in stomachs, I've lost her to the maze, she refuses to build a way out. by now, the streets are slick with garbage and sewer rats, a two-am moon and a haunted bodega full of men who flirt with me like I'm straight, like if they try hard enough, I'll give in. You're talking fast, now, asking if I remember the pride flag and the sidewalk chalk, all I remember is our mothers talking quietly in the other room, the wet calves in the pasture, how you told me you were going to love her so hard it broke your teeth. *What about you?* but it's too late to talk, the grandmother is home, shopping bags cutting into her wrists, she is laughter and lungs, she is dangerous, *nothing about me,* I say, helping with the bags. When the space falls asleep, I take my boxed-up boxer's heart, newly ripped from the chest, and head outside, to the bar where they call me *sugar,* they buy me drinks, they don't ask me about home, or where it hurts, or how long can someone hide until their soul turns into a poltergeist. Instead, we ask each other to dance, and our hands are too busy holding each other's bodies to twist free in the air, we're pressed close, we're glancing at the door every few seconds, an ancient fear, stoked by familial metal and verbal lacerations. *You scar's healing up nicely,* says the bartender who I have a crush on, *Give me another orange slice,* I tell her, and this one she dips in honey and feeds me with a long, gentle reach across the boundary of the bar.

Heist

You, beautiful, with a mother's diamonds
in your pocket, hands full of clear plastic
baggies, blonde hair pulled back with a bobby
pin. We're rolling joints on a faded porch,
we're into rocking chairs in the dull light
of a mostly faded moon, we're uninsured,
nervous, shaking as pieces of burnt toast pass
through our fingers. I want you to bring me
into the vault room so we can make love on
stacks of money, I miss your pink earrings
and the way you blow smoke rings, perfect
circles no matter the occasion, you are auburn
-haired and slick, you miss leaning against
the stoop, you should come home to me but
I don't even know where home is anymore.
I inhale, the joint flaking away beneath heated
pressure, sometimes I'm the fire and other
times I'm an unbrace heart; loyal on the brink
of pink and carmine, this love is rusty, old,
shimmering, thriving only on mist and will.
You ask if I miss it, the life I used to lead,
wondering whether or not I was going to eat
anything other than pasta and pancakes, rain-
slicked lip-gloss bottles, discarded, hiding
in my grandmother's closet, I used to be better
at picking locks. These days I'm hiding behind
barn doors and farm words, my history has been
sealed in seeds-bloomed-scarlet tomatoes. Do you

really think I miss the hothouse, the longing and the
cheek bones, no. Late, maybe midnight, maybe
one-thirty, it's time to close the doors of West
hundred-something street. You tug my coat tail
in a bodega, showing me a large grey cat playing
with a nut. I respond by grabbing your waist.
Couldn't wait? You ask. I feel your grin against
my lips. Tuesday comes and I'm still in bed with you.
My grandmother would have been upset, and I'm
not sure she still would have loved me if I told her.
We hang out in the MET, sitting in the laps of water
nymphs. I'm going to make a new family, I'm going
to teach you how to three-plate carry, I'm going to
love you, open, in the arms of Manhattan.

Peat Moss

She's asking me about the molds
Growing into a patch on my chest
Maybe my heart is failing, the blue
Looks more like a flower or an

Expensive porcelain bowl a mother
Would buy, I wonder if she would
Be interested in my chest mold, if
She'd like to see if I can grow more
Circles of rough, what if one day I

Awake to a weeping willow in the
Center of my lungs, yet aren't I now
Feeding, taking, drinking, loving in
My limbs, hands like anchors drag
Out silt, cuddle with ecosystems of

Ambition, until I am drained of my
Purpose, until I am too much want,
Until I am empty on an evening where
There is nothing left for me to sleep in,

No one left to provide the oxygen, gone
Are forest banisters, I am just another
Parasite who cannot even feed rose
Bushes, no one will drink from caveats

Between my roots, I thought this was
Survival mode, guess it's unsurvival
Of the moss evenings, guess my lungs
Peel apart like popsicle wrappers,
Though my elbows are blue July ice

I am being consumed by red ants, I am
Blowing away in a wind, I am no longer
Beautiful or comfortable, I'm just warm
And scattered, not yet strong enough to
Reach the clouds.

The Winter House

We return to home woods, wool hugs, warm floors, oh how I press
myself hard against the wood to catch a glimpse of your bird. I hear
your laughter from inside the kitchen, how everyone loves you terribly,
how golden you've become, but I

think you were always so true,

> I hope I get you near me, but I'll have to wait until after dinner,
> when everyone's tucked away in pinecone beds, after the last deer
> and rabbit pair have walked into moon, slow and with ease will
> return amber lights

> and gold drinks

do you still care about me?
>> I hold your words in my mouth

>> Latch breath to hitched hands, I care for your love as I
>> would a flame, tease sugar baby beetles into waiting glasses,
>> I am wax, I am inside myself, looking for a way out. Past
>> dusk you join me, cold outside so we talk with our arms
>> around our bodies, I see you seek
>> after birds, cloth-winged watchers in pine clusters, I'm folded

> open-hearted   lying   as dangerous as I've always been

glowing red-coal crushed, pressed tea leaves against chin, catch
me in mittens, pull me against your better judgment. Rules
do not apply anymore, I told you what I told you that day true
midnight passed, knowing it wouldn't be enough, for low inside
my thrumming treasure chest is my final dying secret,

    a catch in the throat, a true ocean, I think you are the laughter and
    the soft press between thighs, you antlered fool, won't you say it
    back, just once, call me rabbit, lungs, split, golden star cakes cool
    on the racks, you are the wire and the fire, softer than the word
    January or starlight.

        Snow is on my hair, cruel how I've lost strength and balance,
        I'm barely passing, won't you warn the forest?

If you leave, I'll need to hide among the pines   nettles sap sticks

    overturned stones, shattered lake and frozen turtles, my life is cold,
    asleep, late. I catch you looking at me, but I can't witness your mouth,
    do my eyes laugh despite it all? Back inside I'm chilled to my ore, curled
    blue sweater hangs over my shoulders. You lean close, doesn't matter
    I'm holding my breath; I want you here. Sometimes I'm a cruel
    button of heat and distress, I'm enamored with winds, tides that
    twist foam into faces, the moon's craters and holes.

so

now what? I'm a catch meant for the fridge, I'm loose as true love's
bite, I'm a latticework of sugar, golden only for you—tell me because
I've forgotten, are your eyes green or brown, do you love inside or
outside helplessness, bites or nail, after the storm breaks or during,
when the sky is filled with wet crows or empty.

Winter Break

Pickled peaches, plums, apple slices, beauty berries, I am letting
my nails echo across your jars. Inside is fire hum, thick carpets, a
kitchen full of our movements, and grace is a bundled flaky heart
that lives on my tongue.

> I'm not in love with you yet, but I could be, for all the times you
> held my hands in your gaze, the too-closeness of the clock, of your
> shoulder pressed to mine, of your private sugars, eyelash on the
> cheek, how you call all the birds *baby* even though you know
> their names.

Gold fabric hangs off your frame   your sleeves are tasseled   I'm constructing

> entire lives to lie you into interest, we fake it for the crowd, do you
> see how many days I won't look at you, I'm afraid you'll catch the
> thrum in my gaze and mistake it for too much heat.

> > It's gauzy-smooth, this crush is crushing me, but I don't
> > mind, my heart will pay for it, believe I am strong
> > enough to withstand you in December. The others are
> > on the porch, watching constellations wink in and out

behind cold pine branches   the floor is coated in navy frost   crisp cones

   a netting of bejeweled needles   all dark green at the base of the old well.

You and I are still inside, making fun of ice, feeding secret cheese bursts to your best friend's dog. I've started to think about you when it's raining, but when I tell you it comes out like I name storms after country songs, I've never been able to commit, I like the shy mouse the best.

I wish the house could sing.

I look forward to the blue-cream sugar cookies, I wonder if I'm strong enough to twist the oven lamps into a crown. If you touch me then you'll know. Instead, you hand me a butter knife and instruct me to tuck it into an already-folded silverware bundle, claiming you'll need a little more sharpness during dinner.

My friend sees me, plum-stained fingers, spotted cheeks, I broke blood-vessels in my jaw from pretending to yawn each time you look my way. What are you doing? My friend asks. My stomach feels like a violin.

Cold Letter Writing

Sending you notes in the lining of
button mushrooms written in gold
gel pen, stamped the secret of January
but soon we'll be stuffing the surface
of each place with chopped baby reds,
crisp tomatoes and burnt egg, maybe
I love sharp champagne cheddar more
than you, bet you didn't think of that,
bet you don't know I throw open the
windows to my house every winter
eve, waiting for you to crawl inside,
blue fire that twists across fields of
roots, you arrive with an open crate
of plum-apples not yet peeled, your
fingers need to be kissed to avoid
frostbite but I'll let someone else
do the job, how much longer must
I pretend I'm not hungry, you've
passed out on a rug my grandfather
knit, I'm on the kitchen floor, crate
overturned, twisting skin from my
teeth, want to stick my mouth in pits
and frost pears, everything is lilac
light and frustrated moon, I've eaten
the forecast, I've banished the sun,
we are all rain and mud and ashes,
we are sleeping in separate rooms
but I'm waiting for you in this corner

of the bed, once I hear you open the fridge it's over, I left you letters in jar linings, wrote your name in a spill of coffee cream on a glass shelf, mushrooms hold my heat but so too do plates of scaled silver-blue cod, a haddock begging for your hands, I've filled the crisper drawers with bitten-back word collections yet you've risen in that damned grey dawn and disappeared into the willows.

no tengo miedo, tengo [s]odio

even though I am running away

       from you in all of my tendons and

sweetbreads, valves breaking

       from the stress, you're looping a finger

in my jeans and I later find

       you're steady inside my heart,

tucked away like a juicy party

       oyster, your neck bears names

of gems, everyone hears your

       face. We're stuck in a grandmother's

house, moist air and old spaghetti

       in the dishwasher, leafy ceiling

calves bucking into my back,

       I switch between crying and

sleeping, I find you lingering

      among leche and paja, you enjoy

molded docks, slim October

      walks, six a.m. swims when fish

still have their tails and you slide

      into barnacle groves, forgetting

the no-talking rule, spilling

      secrets to ridges and molars, please

take the eels and valves from

      my internal curves, the woods

bend towards the lake to create

      a story house, ellos no saben this

is the last time we'll see each

      other, and the family sends us foxes

and beds, a sleepy horse bearing

      wine coolers, we linger between

noise and nonsense, nose to nose, I'm

not talking about how I loved

you faster than I've ever dared, I'm

    smoking your weed and staring at your

mourning mouth, thrums and lungs,

    my nails are laughter and the trees

tie bows and bear bundles of nameless

    peach-hued flowers, I can't have

you without pain, you can't stop me from

    lighting the story box on fire

and I won't stop you from ripping valves

    from my chest, I watch as you

run my ribbons, bragging you're

    rewriting fairytales, you've survived,

able to fall for whoever steps

    in your path, and we're both going to

love again, but at what cost.

Red/Restaurant/Cherry/Father

There is pincushion moss and there is this dizzying red tomato that you slice into thirds, then eighths. I watch you arrange the small red pieces, like checkers, never hearts, until you have created a centerpiece so sweet it turns my cheeks hot. We are in the midst of service, taking care of the indoor plants so they don't grow out of control onto the guest's plates, wrapping rubber bands around our fingers so we don't feel the scald. Will you look after me, after all is said and done?

There are chandeliers with ribbons hanging around their cores, we are careful to avoid the heat lamps, and I don't see the fathers anywhere, I think they have disappeared into the private dining suites so they can discuss wallpaper colors and biscuit consistency. The fathers do not care that I am at dinner, that we are engaging with each other. *You busy?* you ask. I shake my head no. *Do you want to be?* Of course I do, so I take the knife out of your hand and begin to slowly cut into the honey bulbs. They ooze out sweetness, and their hard outer shells are orange as a sun.

It could be helpful if I stayed by your side for the rest of the evening. There is a Saturn loneliness, the kind that you can't store inside of coffee filters or seed bags. The kind of loneliness that turns into a ghost who slams the cabinet doors. This ghost needs a hug. This ghost does not like the color blue.

There are party guests with champagne flutes that look like toys, and someone tells you a rumor, but you only catch the tail-end. There is a bathtub in the center of the room with a small sign next to it that says *don't* and there are boughs of red clay made to look like dough, twisted into galettes, with ceramic blueberries nestled in the center.

I should like to abandon my heart, I tell you. You nod your head, focused on the task at hand. There are true pears to be sliced, never peeled, there are hurts, eyes carved into forks and knives, the restaurant is in full bloom. But I was never meant to return, yet here I am, again and again I hide my body in the space between the registers and the ice cream bar. The servers all know my name, but we are not friends, there is a thunderstorm outside but no lightning, there is something beating in my chest that I don't have a name for, and there is you, taking my hand and tugging me down the hallway towards the cooler.

Where the best cherries are hidden, you say, fishing in the ice, like cold gems the size of fists, betwixt are cherries that remind me of my mother, cherries like the holidays all smelling of well-whiskey. Am I truly at home, with you, or do I just not feel scared when you take my head in your hands? I don't want to return to service. I know there are guests who are hot, guests who don't know how to tie bowties, guests who think they know my name, but they don't. And the lamps are ribbed like pineapples, and the restaurant sign flickers on and off, I am tying and retying my apron as you take the pits from my mouth

Where are the fathers, you ask, and I shrug. *How should I know,* I reply. There are hundreds of fathers, thousands of fathers more, still waiting in the vestibule, for their eldest daughters to return to them. We are busy hiding, we are busy becoming twisted and exhausted beneath disco lights, we are no longer women, and we dislike the fathers.

I was going to return home, to an empty house, but everyone wants me to stay for conversation and chicken. The hours twist: it's late, there are empty beer bottles and a man leaning against the bar with a handful of old popcorn. Soon we will light candles and candies on fire, soon fathers will cheer as we hand them their dinners. I do not

know where the others are, the sisters and the siblings and the parrots. There are no mothers, there is only us and this burning sensation I mistake for love. Rather than telling you how I feel, maybe I could tell you to press right here, into the space between my thumb and forefinger, until the scar disappears. I want soup and I want Band-Aids that don't hurt when I rip them off. I wish my hair weren't green,

I wish I weren't the daughter who threw the confetti, the daughter who hates roses, the daughter with new scars and old scars, stomach aches, grapefruit perfume. I want to be around that summertime feeling, when June and July hold hands, and I forget I have a family

I don't want to be an embarrassment, I don't want to eat cilantro, I don't want to fall in love with mozzarella cheese water and the way you laugh when you're cooking. I begin to forget we are in the kitchen; I forget which stove is the tricky one, which lobster claw is the poisonous one. I am not sorry, and I am not good at telling the truth

Maybe we can leave together and lay on the embankment. There will be stars whose names we can't remember, and these stars will be hidden behind the clouds. Loud and blue yellow enter the lightning bolts into the sky, but we aren't going to get burned, we aren't beautiful enough to be turned into gods.

Soon it is twelve, soon I am sorry I am not around as often

as I would like, soon we walk out in a pack of twenty-five, each of us modeling the three-plate carry, some of us wearing bags slung over our shoulders that are filled with iced wines, dripping a thin trail of cold like an irritated and rude slug, but it doesn't matter because the fathers are impressed, the room is glorious, there is no imposter syndrome, there is no love, there is only a thin veil of separation between their plates of food and the knife which severs the meat.

marimo

consider the ripped green strips of holiday tinsel
now peeled apples, I watch your hands gripping
the tools, I want to take your wrists and show you
they look just like my wrists, my hands, instead
I put my head on a fist and ask your husband about
his algae obsession. Maybe there's nothing wrong
with a little linkage, doesn't algae create a feeding
web, don't you have space in your heart for another
person's love? It's my fault. I am the one who wants
to feed the ecosystem, to hold all the flaking winged
hearts in all the hands and shoulders and hair ties, I
want to bundle our mutual sparks in red elastic bands
screw green I'm talking low, lean, thrum colors, I want
all of you to love all of me all of the time. Maybe I'm
asking too much. I dislike your group because I want to
be there too, when waking in winter dark you rise from
dreams, exhausted, padding faded slippers to the fridge
I want to be reading in low lamp light, I want to ask if
you'd like me to heat your milk on the stove.

Promise

I lose track of august in sobbing and if
you really wanted to save me you could
have done so already, instead we're
eating hot berries off mother's stove
juice dripping like fangs, clinging like
morning-blue pearls, I tell you I'm sick
of trying to save my own life and you
pat me on the shoulder as if to say, it's
all going to be okay, you can endure
beyond what is deemed reasonable, we're
talking about surviving the men and
the wolves, the salvation tactics and
whatever they think is cool these days
all slime jackets and bonfire teeth, I
don't want to survive, I want to be blue
as a mold spore, maybe I could turn
into a navy-haired horse, I'd be good
as the day the sun stayed away just
enough to let us make forts in the sand
I tried to defend myself against his
hands but it didn't matter, isn't this
how the story always goes, turning
to each other and asking if this is how
that story goes, yes, so we go on, to
survive, to eat meals with each other
without threats or promises, we are

protecting one another I guess I just
wish I could have told you back then,
that I wasn't an urchin or a person, I
needed someone to take one look at me
and know that I'd been robbed and
I know salvation is a joke we pass on
the porch, like we can maybe save
each other if we're being gentle enough
but listen, what I meant to say earlier
was I didn't think you could save me
back then I made my heart a spiked
and poisonous thing, they kept coming
for me, hiding out in the woods and
tugging my waist near the lake, I know
you know. I hate that we barely fit under
the cover of love.

Pink Velarium

Strawberry-covered canopies, champagne cheddar, Bischoff
crust, mint, the other girls watch us pretend we're not in love.
I am not hungry for another seven-hour dinner, flaking honey-
hued chairs, soft shoes, won't you take my hand when the
others aren't looking. Wind inflates the table cloak, there
are butter knives with *lord* printed on the handles, each
plate bears a feather stamp, I am reminded of my partner, how
she told me I knew more than I let on.

I am aware you adore spice, you're hungry for the head chef
who gently smirks when you catch her eye. There are crystal
bowls of pink and pearl cantaloupe, canopy poles are coated in
pale grey ribbons, the day is clouded, the lakes are short, we
are so many other than I, who else would ever dare?

Curved like an eyelash, the too-green avocado is stamped with
two words, *betray us*, and I am hardly breathing, I have a crush on
the salmon, I am drinking bear wine, the left corner of the canopy
contains a smudge of grease. Next come the bones, proof of stock
and boil and heart and pastel tomatoes and fall and fry and stew,
there is soup, there is meat on the stove, there is a thin separation
and a toast.

I wait for the dip that never comes, catch you tugging at ribbons
in the outdoor kitchen, you want to unravel the place where her tongue
and her lungs hold hands, you want to smother me, you want parted

lips and king fish, first fins and tuna tails, fake love and a play about life, yes you might win her over, and I must stop myself from unlighting the fires, breaking the lamps, I hide the *God* silverware, I want to cover my eyes.

Bothered in the middle of the shift, bored lamb, I replace pepper flakes with rose confetti but no one minds, I'll find someone new to pull my wool apart.

I see her, clove in one hand, juggling soup bowls in the other, do I tell her I'm desperate, do I admit I'm hungry too, do I leave my worship in the pantry? But she catches my eye and smiles. I slowly take your hand from my hip and follow her into your house.

Dicentra

Winter

I am in love with the sous-chef & her flower bundles she brought for a candy special, I watch as she coats peach and lilac in a thin cloak of sugar, she wears arrows in her ears, and I feel bad my arms are empty. I peel nail polish from my cuticles, I am as lost as I was months ago, when all this first began, my heart is always too affected by food, I have recurring dreams about organs coated in apple skins and necklaces of pear seeds, I wake starving, I can't remember if it's December or spring, I don't want to be alone.

Spring

I wonder if she would go with me, to the forest of yellow-green leaves, we could talk about their resemblance to butternut squash, we could be lit I used to walk through sprinklers at night, I sat on guard rails and ran around the woods behind the house, I never knew my way around the sand, but I didn't have to, there was always someone near to hold the flashlight as we walked through the night. I wish I could listen to bird songs while we cook, instead I am humming and helping with the honey jars, there is a breeze from the back door, the wood is chipping and it's just as well, this building is faded, smells vaguely of sunscreen and salt, we lay our bacon out to dry on the back porch, will she recognize me after time has passed?

Summer

June nights I have a dream I try to put mascara on. The brush accidentally touches my nose and flowers begin to spill from my face. I doodle the word *bloom* on the insides of my fingers, I think about your heart for hours. Maybe my memories are meant to be doughy in the summertime, what month is it anyway? I'll lay out my feelings and flaky croissant-dough hearts one by one on the table until I figure out what is true and what is merely a result of the season. I still don't know what I'm trying to say to her.

Fall

It's late, an evening. When she asks for help I follow her into the walk-in freezer with a crate, standing quiet as she loads the box with begonias, clover, fuchsia, hollyhock, linden, roses, bundles of sugar cubes bound in cloth, a wine made of sunflowers, edible glitter, six ribeye steaks, a chilled butcher's knife with the words *hello, heaven* etched in the side, overripe cherries, salted cream, fudge, hummingbird cake, sesame oil, an oyster that someone has written on with sharpie— that says *love* that I think we both pretend not to see, and a bottle of horseradish, and a vial of gold flakes, and a jar of tomato sauce, and a glass orb whose ingredients need to be shaken up in order to braid together.

Green Cherries

We reach the lake at dawn. Crowded with blooms of algae and freshwater mussels, I see you are distracted by coral-hued snakes, weeping willows feeding from the left bank, the house just beyond, coated in mists of this dawn. I want to ask you to pause, to swim, to turn violets into knots. Instead, we carry on towards the others.

You joke that the house is haunted, and our friends are more like poltergeists than comedians. *What kind of ghost am I*, I ask, unable to keep the love behind my mouth. I catch your lips quirk at the sides. You laugh as I swear beneath the ivy tendrils, but why is the house shrouded in green when the windows are all cracked, are there creatures of the forest already stuffed in my chest, will I sleep in a field of nightmares, will you hold me so I don't sink?

The others are on the back porch, drinking amber ales and eating ribbon cake. The closer I stand to you, the closer I am to collapsing in on myself like an ancient star. I wonder if my heart glows red despite all this hiding, I wonder if you mind the red birds.

We sit close, there's not enough space. There are crinkled cookies and red velvet cheesecake, a platter of berries, knots, a promise, a pit of frosting and a box of truffles printed with the word *cold* over eight dozen times. Do you lose your breath at me, do your hands prefer pinecones, do you know how to heal yourself? Could you heal me, too?

I want to ask if you know I am haunted, must you bring up ghosts at the dinner table, could you count clear sugar bubbles as tangible spirits or are you too focused on the heartbreaking blue ribeye and its chilled core, do you remember where lungs came from when our host serves us dishes tinted navy, do you cry at the seashell coconuts, the primrose lobster, the diver whose broken heart almost drowned her yet she survived to bring us this buttermilk bisque, a crate of deep-bellied bowls and woody honey Henry roes, I bet she's given her ghosts to the cods, you know the Atlantic has secrets whose depths a human could never plumb, but a ghost? Surely a ghost has lived, swam, twisted into a mild-mannered snowflake crab, a wheel from the front, a charm bracelet, you're twisting my feelings into a confidential confit, you're staring across the table at me as I tell stories of my own ghosts who haunted my family long before I knew I too was followed.

You're not the only one, you say, twisting a platinum knife around your plate. *I have a story about ghosts*, interjects another guest, and I place my tongue between my teeth and pretend I don't care about spring, if it helps, I'll denounce every pear and fern, no more rescue-sea foam or needy olives, not this lonely crocodile, oh was I wrong. And it's not about green or ghost or even love. Maybe I am lonely, maybe I won't finish dinner. Perhaps I'd love to be anything other than an open and obvious wound, including but not pertaining to: a radish, a rush, a cinnamon stick, a less-salty sea, burnt scallop, a crush, a statue, an unfairness, a poltergeist, baby, a loud and haunted starfish, or is purple more the hue of haunt and frightening evening. But before I fade into my own after-dinner coffee mug, will you tell me what color you think your eyes are. After years of gazing, I find out I still don't know. If I were to guess, and yes, this list is me avoiding telling you something—frankly, anything—I'd think cherries, or maybe apple cider, the despair and the twisted storm, not the cobalt of your bracelets but maybe a lovely, once-in-a-lifebeat moon, maybe sometimes hot coal and other days peat moss in the shape of a spell.

I know you see me, but I want to remain hidden. I take everyone's dishes to the sink. Oh, the longing to be back at dessert, twisted with the ghastly ghost-pink want of being the plate and the spoon, but I've never been fond of cherries or anything with a pit, and if you ever got the courage to reach into my chest, take out my heart and you'll sooner find it's a strawberry pincushion than a room of valves. What can I say. I'm a liar and afraid of heaven, I'm a writer hiding behind her wishes, I'm thinking about your irises, I'm drunk on words, sweets, the forest, you, leaning in the doorway of the kitchen, asking if I'd like a hand.

Ocean Crush

auburn eggs flecked with gold rest in bowls on the mantle, I try not to break wine glasses, I am looking for a space to hide my body while the guests dance across the living room, people are in love at the dining room table and I am hiding my face, hot from a glance at the back of your head,

you're dressed like a sea captain again and I must put a hand over my mouth to stop myself from asking you about the waters, were there domino-patterned octopus, a light gold starfish that steals hearts, your vanilla cologne bottle emptied of its contents, accidentally overboard, I imagine you

bent over the hull, reaching into the depths but all you find are mellow yellow mermaids born of the moon, I bet the evening was warm as cake batter, I bet you'd call me a fawn and the town on the coast would call us old-gold, we don't use the *l*-word here, it's all metallic hues, my earrings

like starbursts, the ache in my chest in the kitchen, there is a harvest in the fridge and when we sit down to dinner, I am near apricot bread, my fork and knife are rusted and stamped with the words *love you*, someone quips about how adoration silverware has gone out of fashion and you shake your head,

you tell the guests these metals with which we eat were forged from discarded sea masts, we're participating in saving the lives of coral, but I'm distracted by the image of snapped ships on your gold-button blazer, I want to know who ordered the words, why am I the only one holding a fork that says *love*, and the woman next to me complains that her spoon says *candy cane*, why don't the Fates play tricks with her instead? she reaches across the table and toys with the bracelet on your wrist, uninscribed? she asks. I'm just waiting for the right words, you say, glancing over at me.

The table angles itself towards your hands as you tell a story about a harpoon cutting through the middle of your boat, you almost drowned but someone—or something—dragged you back to shore, and the table toasts to your savior, but I'm not there, I'm hiding oars beneath my bed, I'm

stuffing a wet sweater in the dryer, there are sea urchins growing in the tub and you can see the water alight through my window, the moon is wondering why I don't just tell you, I'm about to return to the party when I hear a knocking at my door, you're standing in front of me with carmine

in your cheeks, you're handing me my locket, half-broken, half-coral, a solitary remnant from the night I jumped in to save you from the waves, oxblood red, you were passed out as I tended to your wounds, you stained my foyer, you're asking if I'd like to leave the party to go for a walk along the shore.

Summer

We go for a walk. And I'm in love with, but don't want to tell. I think about you, in states never been, wonder if you'd give me pennies from your pocket, hot from the sun, so I could wish on a fountain. We could be wishes, too, and witches and stars, we could never leave, defy the breeze and the fates, we could be floating above a volcano, our faces reflecting bubbles built from the mantle, I wonder if I would still look good in the lava. My heart is an arcade, rainbow and full of tickets, still beating so long as you feed gold coins into the slot, I operate when you are not around, but I miss you, could you write when I'm gone? Let me know if you ever took down the reeds, found freshwater oysters, a pebble that says *sometimes*, a discarded book on the bench, that you remember me, me, me?

You told me you'd like to be forgotten. I've never met anyone who I'd like to stick around most. I have these clocks I've made; I keep track of the leaving, I don't want to make a clock for you, I want to go see the great blue owls gathering in the field downtown, I want to write letters on ticket stubs that say *hello, do you miss me*, and *daydream*. I'll send the owls away, a wingspan echoing *what I've lost, violet wine wins again, I tried not to look at you during dinner,* and *I care about you.* You might unwrap a *can you tell, do we stay, would you swim first or me.*

I return home. I don't know if you will remember me when I'm gone. The plan was always to leave, I never thought I'd want to stay. I want to tell you it's tree roots, the yellow cherry I took a picture of and texted to you, it's change, it's this color green I can't name, it's exhausted and it's a fire where we both get space to warm our hands. I'm here and I'm hidden, sealed away my adoration in mud puddles and hurricane flowers. I could tell you. We could go swimming instead.

I have a crush on a bog

They dress us with crows, my heart is a glittering onion and my veil
barely stays on my face, these days are liquid-long, crawling up, desire
appears on my windowsill, a many-winged bug, I want to tell you
I had a nightmare again last night, that I lost you in grey-green bog
water, you disappeared into the mouth of a crocodile, told me it wasn't

a big deal because you love toothy alphabets, tattoos on your thumbs
only, you can come back if you want, bring forth brine bracelets, branches
filled with birds whose projects are sequin-focused cross my mind with
wicking details, I promise I'll let you talk about raisins. I'll stick my
feet in the pond even though I'm scared. We can be here for a few days

a few hours, a few more good years, celebrations will be filled with confetti
holographic and green, each shape a beautiful cutout of cranes, carrots
silver fish then sparkling roses, the lovely pale fires we once snuffed out
with our sweatshirt sleeves, we can turn our memories to stamps, send
effort in salt pails, write some love letters, I wear your consumer's claws

around my neck, I feel home when we're sitting by the shore near bark
twists, do you feel me watching the water or are you over my crush, but
do you want to wear a chandelier, for weed and rose queens, do you want
to make the bees jealous, your hair is blush sometimes lobelia cardinalis
other days I'm in jeopardy and your crimson birds tell me you like being

a ghost, they can hear you outsinging their feelings in early evenings, we
miss you but you're busy, no orchid-and-arrow at my back but I can feel
you, your aim is perfect your eyes are acorn and gramineus, do you still feel
euphoria at the sight of water, do you still hate tentative soil, do you know
what a breeze feels like against the back of your neck? For the sake of bogs,

the bags, the jersey girls and waiting honey-infused pitchers, do you feel rich now you're digested, do you feel loving now you're a nutrient, have you become a plant tissue, can you stop me crying? It's early spring and I'm reminded of drowsy days when you laced your fingers through the ocean's harness, no venus yet I'm still trapped, I'm supposed to return home like

nothing ever happened, and you're supposed to cast a proper haunting flood, your waters are cranberry bogs and you're appealing to everyone the problem was never your beauty, it was your lack of desire to eat me it was your obsession with left-handed toothy protectors, yes that winter I fell in love again, but my heart only knows your name, I accidentally told

on myself in the county diner, I'm being hunted by the others and you're not even brave enough to whistle a goodbye my way. I might have been brave once, I might have told you I hate when you grow out of control, you don't care, you're multiplying rosemary puffs and secret quartz fox in trap crates you're not tolerant of locks, this is your zone, my-my caroliniana, please keep

the gators at bay, I promise I'll take off my boots before I enter your sacred waters, I'm unarmed but not unharmed, I'm ready to bloom into a nightmare a cool little thing, they don't know I can overwinter my way out of storms, but if it was just you and I, don't you think we could grow different this time?

Kitchen as Memory

Us, bent over the counter during pre-meal, listening to you
rattle off the ingredients for this week's specials. Foamy smoke

from the fisherman's stew curling into the air. Sweet, tomato-
orange broth, shining and newly cleaned muscles, vague outline

of a purple and white shell that once hid a scallop. The scallop,
floating in the stew, my hand inching towards the crisp, thin

bread slice hiding just beyond the other servers' line of sight.
When I catch your eye, you raise your eyebrows. *Don't,* you

mouth, and we both know you're right.

The dreams begin after the restaurant closes. I have left, books
stuffed in cars, journals full of stained dupe papers, your goodbye-

card taped to the inside of a journal. I can see the restaurant on my body.
Hot plate burn on my right hand, thumb bending too far, nights I wake

covered in sweat, faded memories of floors covered in mushrooms
and upturned nails. There are dreams of love, of your hand skinning
a beautiful silver fish.

I pressed my stomach against a table, I was seduced by the maple glaze,
I waited, eyes glossed over, loving the curl of carrot as it was peeled again
and again, until only the core was left.

I am haunted in kitchens I have no attachment to, I dutifully wrap takeout, the floor everywhere is cold. I cry over the loss of a building I lay no claim in.

I begin dreaming of us, together, on a boardwalk. The river is full of cranberries. Before I wake up, I trip into the water and drown.

This is just to say goodbye

heads of lettuce, dupe receipts, a new server notebook, farewell recipes hidden among the bookshelves, blue light of the diner, bye grease pencils, your letter, love, candy spools, cracker crust, so long *I know better*, oceans, a drawing of your fisherman's stew, godspeed gauze in the sleeve, discarded pearls in buckets, blue clover, goodbye to the private netting of algae hearts in the parking lot, the swan song playing through a faded red radio drowning in the kitchen sink, song of my heart, I'll miss lust, sycamore trees, low drama and thin farewells, blue peaches, jaws, the way I used to open fish stomachs, oil, goodbye to the knives and the handles, deception, red egg yolk twists, bye lip bite, bodega cat keeping track, paws and thumbs, empty jars, godspeed cinnamon and thyme, red carpets, fungus, sleeping beneath tables, so long talented turquoise shells, tripped mussel lungs, rag-doll lettuce, so long were the rainy Tuesdays, the hallway to the mystery freezer, swans long for your hands to warm their hearts, animals asleep at your station, godspeed ladies, lime rinds in locked boxes, plastic doors, blue bins, stuffing, farewell lilac crab bundles, warnings, bird calls, burnt bread, richness, autumn, bye onions in fire, duck breast without the duck, glaze, morning, muscle, goodbye milk crates, jokes, blue grief and blue lobster, my legacy, a pastry, goodbye to the booths by the windows, old apples, ribeye cores, shaved truffle, so long doorbell, prized caramel crusted cod, vanilla lattice, trustworthy carrots, bye bite of my heart, mollusk in the morning, peas-turned-cabbage, mothers, the song through the speakers singing about sisters, bye witches, dry storage, trust, farewell scallops, butternut squash, fraught flowers, fighting in the bathroom, godspeed frosted candy hearts spilled in February aprons, display cases, good wine, godspeed creamy peach forests, the martinis I dropped, the hounds and the homes, goodbye to your speech about being better than me, raspberry crème brûlée crushes, farewell crepe paper and fake pine trees all in a row, silver ornaments, turquoise ice, so long fifties folded up like twenties, the time I had to charge seven dollars for oranges, swan your way out of my heart, why don't you ignore the rotary phone, sit still for the bye and the jars full of rutabaga confetti, the faded CDs in your truck, green crates, bye tangos, Frank Sinatra for the regulars, lemon drops and sugar rims, your laugh, godspeed and don't forget to save the lights beneath the bar, save the mirrors, save the swan- soft chef coats with their thirteen stamped buttons, every bear has a soul, steal goodbye from my hands, steal crates of beer from the fridge, please give me the so-long I've been dreaming of the moment you tell me it was all worth it, the farewell to end all farewells, the bye not caught in the throat, say goodbye, and say you love me, say godspeed and say you'll stay, so long as I am in the freezer say you'll save me the swans, they're so cold and delicious, this is just to say I hate farewell.

Assuming a forest won't stay the same

rooting around pastures for clover
sunset like green goddess sauce
muscles ache I've lost track of heaven
my hair is a bun of twigs, I can't recall
the last dandelion, sauce will be sweet
stop recalling the way she bit her lip,
her crying and your lying, *siempre estás*
con hambre, doesn't matter, you touch and
scrape by on family mealtime grew a new
lawn on the back porch, harvested freshwater
sharks whose eyes reflect nail polish and damn
these woods, *nadie* sabe *nada* but at least
you've kept your heart at a swooping pastel
pastern the reeds have been gathered in buckets
and folktale water begins to flood clicking and
biting your feet, you see her at the mouth of
the jaws of the jaws of the forest and for a second
you are dreaming, she isn't really there she's
making resin tables on Madison Avenue, she's
in scratched red sneakers in the back of someone's
van, snorting lines of coke off a ruby guitar, or
maybe she *estácomiendo un corazón sin dientes*,
maybe sleeping beneath a pile of cable knit
sweaters she stole from a recently-seduced
sea captain, or perhaps she's kissing the receiver
of the last payphone in Manhattan, either way,
it's end-of-the- road startle, it's brittle love

and young potatoes, she's not really here, you're
imagining the scent of clove and why wouldn't you
you're in a field of clover, but the others stop
their work, some pause with the edible flower
buckets poised mid-pick, others have tripped
over roots and lay on their sides in disbelief
others still are leaning against trees like they're
coaxing them straight from the earth, and she is
walking towards you, arms outstretched, a mess,
you wake up elevated in a cloud of grief, birdsong
is floating through an open window like a promise.

Surge

I wake and can't grasp hold of the
day. The fridge, blue and pale,
hums. Outside, sea-stones rise out
of the water like flower buds

each salty, coated in circles, urchin
spores, bird feathers. I am raw and
restless on the coast, obeying my
mother's orders to not poke

the jellyfish, why must I always
press into pain, she used to beg me
to stop hurting with my thumbs
until she too turned, with her

metallic blue eyeshadow, stained
cross necklaces, her eyebrows
are beautiful, she once gathered
mollusks in jars, never has any

discs stuck on her slim fingers, nails
coated in red, I push my own hand
out to the horizon and pretend we
are one, together to grab

the curl of surf, and to be clear this
is before I knew she loved me, this
is before the empty house and the
witness, the year of oatmeal

fires, amber shutters growing mold
off the half-moon desk, clouds
were fingernails and fingernails
were hazy, my hand turns

blue from water's glow, similar
in hue to the lake we bottled and
stored for emergencies, I was never
good at filling jars without at

least a filing's worth of algae blooms,
each green and oxygenated, in
my childhood thought algae held
hands with willows, believed

so many things to be true about my
life, only later as an adult did I find
out there were lies then came holes,
what I can describe as

pockmarks in memory, a lace doily
of grey matter, each opening like a
chance or a promise. The kitchen is
all circle structures and

ceramic cows. Rounded-out mugs,
azure with fake gold flakes, cereal
bowls full of berries, the opening of
a cherry missing stem

eyes of the old grey cat sleeping in
the warm patch, I leave everything
behind. I thought she might return.
I don't tell mother

about the ghosts, how she arrives
in dreams with penny buns in one
hand, wicker basket in the other,
her wedding ring is lost to

the sand, I wake up starving and
wishing I were a season or a storm,
no longer woman but séance or
small, soft god. No longer

man, but butterfly property, a wave
goodbye to October, the courage to
mean it, the minnow statues in the
doorways, goodbye

to everything smelling like nuts
and wet stones, no more poppyseed
muffins cooling on the table, I lock
myself out of my

own heart, I sell the car, I become
sunburnt and lush, drinking wine
in the middle of the day. Come late
three, then four, dream

I bite my own neck, I split open the
past with a wave of my hand, knock
coasters to the floor, and letters on
napkins, a scarf she knit

using blue yarn only, a picture of
a letter, not even the letter itself,
detailing all the ways in which she
felt hollow inside, like a worm

or a party favor. Down the street
someone is walking towards me.
She has sea urchins tattooed on her
hands, she keeps water statues

in the foyer, dances for fun. If I
didn't have breathing problems
none of this would have happened.
We could be strangers beneath

neon lights, holding each other in
a strip of rainbow, there is a pastry
chef deep-frying caramel and blt
sandwiches, above our

heads is a little red pizza symbol,
we'll never give each other a chance,
we can be playful and hazy, I won't
tell you about my

mother and you won't, yours.
Imagine us now, the street is just a
street with no rain, the lights shine
in a way they are supposed to.

Someone with a mother shape and
mother form texts me to ask how I
am, she is an entryway, alley arch,
door without a knob. I

won't love anyone too much. Then
the chef hands me a greasy paper
plate containing what he claims to
be his rendition of a New

York City pizza slice. We lock
eyes for a moment, and I wonder
if he has any scars or tattoos, he'll
eventually cover up. I want to

ask him if he ever clutches his heart
on the bathroom rug, where air
smells of mold and soil. Instead,
our fingers brush. He doesn't

nod, I don't speak, and we both
turn back to a line of strangers.

Concord Blue

I've run out of ways to explain
the way the ice turned blue that day
how hot your hand felt in mine,
protecting me from a shallow lake

tucked away into the earth, we use
trees to steady the path, I think I
might not mind if I tripped if you
were by my side, your felt coat

full of half-broken buttons, crumpled
cigarette box in your pocket, I know
you miss red lips, you miss crooked
pasts and robbing flower gardens

you took naps on the hood of your car
left the windows open in a rainstorm,
reckless beautiful you, I'm not but so
desperate for your return, let's finish

this walk with our heels intact, no
azure wings for me, though the birds
echo their disapproval, they've stayed
the migration, they eye us from half-

empty trees, ahead are evergreen pines
whose sap I used to enjoy, the sticky
that comes with being so green, flower
goo, as my mother used to call it, even

though no flowers grow here, it's just
us and a frosted pathway, running the
clock, we'll be hand-in-gloved hand
until inevitably you are pulled away

from me, your eyes the color of lake
ice, she takes you by the heart and off
you go, disappearing into a warmer
life, but I wonder if you miss snow

if you long for seasons, do you miss me
when it rains, I'll be here, turned to blue
stone, this isn't a folktale, please be sure
to return home with me in your pocket.

In another universe you stay and we do each other's hair for the wedding

Arguing about what chiffon really means, we in pale
    blue silk pajamas, everything is seductive, the ants

are recluses until we bring out the cakes, I remember I saw
    your arms up to the elbows in batter once, thought,

you are my home, now I say, why stay, the grandmothers
    are gone and the kitchen is a sword, your ex hums

in the foyer and your mother is pitching a fit over her makeup
    leave it all behind, I say goodbye to you in the daffodils

but you never followed me out here and to begin with I shouldn't
    be hanging in the brush, it's fire season and my heart

is weak as matches and a wick, I've given up the knives and
    forks with embossed flowers, let's divide this old house

in two, you must leave the space in my chest where you once
    built a nest, please don't ever try to hold me again with

the same hands, please know I've learned and unlearned cloud
    formations, the sticky daisy patterns in the diner downtown

we are actors and I'm wearing pearls, an embroidered leaf dress
    I let my body climb out of my resting suit, I let you have

stories about scars and tongue depressors, you learn to call
        a heart a heart and the moon stays a moon but you won't

know my face when it's old; forgive me, for I have never been
        the same woman twice.

Smooth Green Snake

Next comes low light, centipede you couldn't kill,
rain peeling the sides the house, buildings lean
forward, needle-like and green-gold, porch lantern
swing, pool overflow, you think again of sanguinity

in the bed, the pitch and the shed, no-one forms a hole
in the doorway, they swing and sink your mind is sulfur
you're getting lost in looseness and evening, bedsheets
and somewhere a ball of twine, gray photo of retired

racehorses, a bottle of wine, also green-gold, half-empty
on the floor. While kindling the deal a God did you ever
think to ask her to save your own life, too? You asked the
doorway to shift into two, for your eyes to stop fraying at

light, for the tiles in his bathroom to stop their spinning, gauzy
and yellow, sixties style just like she wanted, what's a gazebo
got on a basement, doorway range and stair arch, you follow
outside is thunder, you think yes, of course, you think, cross-

cut, again with the odysseys and heroes, singing then calling
the exes slouched against their doorways, empty space, the
absence of a lover, does a man become a hero, do you
become gorgeous or gorgon, the monsters were cutthroat

meaning cut at the throat, or, across many throats, snake
coats, an intersection of mud and flutter, grass patches
all yellow and begging for sacrifice, you should have taken
bundles of hair, discarded bottles, a small piece of a voice

you are called a hag, you are called a jewel, you are tempted
with soft tissues and sweetbreads, ignore the cousins in the
moss court down the street, your mind becomes a lightless
ditch, a twisted heel, let's total the hammers and harpies

now harps, this fabulous storm ripping open stomachs
of roadkill, maybe I'm yours, I return to the tub every time
and imagine someone is cradling my body in the water
I ignore warnings of electricity in the pipes, sting of soap

low-hanging faucet, please lift the sword above your head
practice in the mirror before cutting out the heart of a father
drunk on the idea of memory, will they remember or will
they call you a horror, banish you into a tightly wrapped

forest. Sycamores form and through the arches walk wolves
why compare their jaws, why romanticize teeth as play and
tongue as drip, rip, pin-sharp clip, they witness your awful
wingless body floating to the sky, no one will tell you when

it's your turn to lift the weapon, drop your sword in the old
sand, they'll tell stories of you, daughter as driftwood, not
yet cool enough to be compared to candy or wheels, ribbons
or wax lips, this is the way a sun forms through the trees

there was bloodshed—whose? —it all comes down to howls
bundled in cheesecloth, stories about naming your parents
and when you return home, you find not a light switch but
a tooth.

During which I make up a series of lies
for you in August

For example, it's the end of July and the moon is in my backyard again. I turn into a very small bird and haunt you. I am a rotten peach and a worm-filled jam jar. I didn't eat the last of your jelly seeds and even though you told me you wouldn't leave the windows tossed open during a storm, your ex's perfume lingering in the foyer, told me you'd stop smoking yet draped over the walls are small silver ghosts, even after the argument in the berries—patchwork of pink-red-blood from crow beaks, half-eaten smeared raspberries and those little red berries which are poisonous but whose name I forgot, yes—even after all that, I am not a person. I am a drama, I am your Sunday, sand below lightning, wave that makes you hate the sea, darling but not yours, don't love you. Could let go any time. Want to turn the cheese into moons, water into limes, did you know I used to be a monster? I begin to wonder how long confessions go on before the priest gets tired and walks away.

Tell me you want to know and we'll go from there

Hazy days. Everywhere green, muggy, vegetable fields encircled by pines, reminds me of the times we walked near fields of wheat, monarch butterflies, still loved each other, didn't mind highway overpasses, strangers on bicycles, a stray grey cat wrapping its body around legs, the times I went to parties and couldn't enter unless I took all my clothes off. The house with the sharks, the chef with sun tattoos on both his knees, she came with me back then, we couldn't be together, we belonged to the men, so many of us clustered around each other at the edge of the jellybean pool. Bitter, couldn't swim in the expensive water, outcast, eating too many empanadas by the stove, never learned to sew but quick with a needle and skin, railroad tracks, cat claws, praying in the bathroom for breath to return to my lungs. Wonder what you'd do if you knew. Isn't this always how it goes? Warm bar, beer is average, I want them to love me but realize loving means knowing, and knowing is distrust, times I sold tech and gold, have so many rivals I can't go home without hiding, could only pay waitresses in pennies and nickels until work picked up, do you want to know about the times I ran out of clothes, stole from cheerleaders, pocketed statues of blue cows and ice-clear birds, roses blown from glass, a necklace passed down from many grandmothers, learned to read stamps on silver, first I'll need you to adore me, then we can talk about the blood.

Mellow

The kind of crush that makes you believe in
peppermint again, strawberry of a Saturday,
oatmeal in father's bowls, tomato tub, sprite
instead of starling, not human or woman,
just yolk, berry milk, vanilla-banana,
butter-flour and lobster-oyster, you're afraid
of joy, you don't want to share, you want
eggs, comfort, a place to hang a pea coat,
to fall into bed together, the too-haunted
house off the coast with hickory spiders,
sea foam licking clean the shore, letters you
wrote to your ex, all eaten by candles. Enter
love, jellyfish, combs, discarded phone, the
memory of breakups taking the form of
ghosts, the time you almost choked and
died, hid in the powder room with the
blue jars and ground pepper, what happens
to the dogwood tree after it is torn apart,
what happens to your heart when it is no
longer capable of withstanding your past,
baby, everything is false. You want him to
hold your face in his hands but you're too
jagged, sea ice is different than lake ice, who
cares, the hunters still hide in the forests,
lately it's blue pines at all hours, wearing his
jacket again, told yourself this wasn't love
but lately you care too much.

Season Bonding

Stop / the sun is coming / do you ever trust hands to hold you / eat the confetti / spin / acorn / bed / the day is ash / there are so many ways to say *green* / do we tell them about infatuation / how to teach a human about love / how should we care / why the never-ending sea / when the cove meets the rocks / stay / this stick is to write notes in the sand / this breakfast is to discuss the break before the breakup / high heels / orange paint / Saturday is summertime all over again / there is laughter / there is a naturally grown tomato / unbothered / rolling around the mouth of a wolf / like a candy / or a human drug / every version of an animal is perfect / every time I sing I turn red / winter won't find us here / am I creating the circumstances for love / it is not necessary to touch lone needles / to sit on hot roofs / just eat leftover seeds / no / not today / I've had tea for the first time / my instinct is always to leave / maybe this time we'll stay / you're here, too / under the soft humming oak / willow trees have wilting spiders / plants drink from the lake / and the algae forms a living / breathing / network / don't disturb the surface / don't go near the ducks / swans sweet and transforming into girls / the girls run through fields in white dresses / there is no presence of threat / the myth has died / the color blue no longer means death / the grip of a man can't happen here / violence is when my mouth is broken / back to the girls / young women all safe and barefoot in the crooked forest / stomachs full of pomegranate seeds / did you know I will eat every fruit / I miss Manhattan pretzel / I too will become a young girl / free / will you come with me / this existence is bliss / there is no hurt / tomorrow I won't / exist.

Late Night

You are in his bathroom
again, sitting on the tub's cold
edge, marveling at his wife's
efficiency, the way she hung
gold and silver stars on the
ceiling, the tinsel lining the
doorway, someone's drunken
lipstick kiss on the mirror. You
wore blue on a whim, painted
wings on the backs of your
hands, just in case you wanted
to fly away. Your shoes hurt,
your cigarette is burned down
to the heat. They had horses
at the wedding. They have a
red refrigerator. You open the
window and look out at New
York City.

Acknowledgments

Many thanks to the following literary journals where several of these poems first appeared, in various forms:

The Amazine – "La Amapola"

Anti-Heroin Chic – "Windy Blue Nights" and "And in July I am losing track of myself near a tide pool"

Beaver Mag – Pink Velarium

The Bitchin' Kitsch – "antes"

Blue River Review – "Hull"

Cutbow Quarterly – "This isn't another story of how we counted money in Hell, but it could be"

Delicate Friend – "Cold Letter Writing"

Dogwood Alchemy – "During which I make up a series of lies for you in August"

Ethel Zine – "Green Suns" and "Winter Break"

Euonia Review – "Apartment Problems" and "Green Goddess"

the gamut mag – "Manhattan, again"

The Gone Lawn – "Eldest Daughter," "I have a crush on a bog," and "To Fortify the Ingredients"

The Hungry Ghost Project – "late Tuesday"

Harvard Square Press – "Season Bonding"

Invisible City – "Grief Birds"

JAKE The Anti-Literary Magazine – "During which the witches descend into the haunted house together"

Kiss Your Darlings – "Ocean Crush"

Last Leaves Mag – "If you're reading this, I still love you"

Lover's Eye Press – "Surge"

The Lumiere Review – "Goldfield"

Maitri Poetry – "no tengo miedo, tengo [s]odio"

the museum of americana – "sea/salt/sugar/phones"

The Nassau Review – "Soft Livestock Threat"

orangepeel mag – "Dicentra," "Red/Restaurant/Cherry/Father," and "Summer"

Pastel Pastoral – "Peat Moss"

Penumbra Press – "I wake up each week / just to head towards you" and "my family doesn't know I'm queer / at least the ocean does"

Raleigh Review – "Late Night"

Red Ogre Review – "There are parties in the second layer of hell, but I don't go anymore"

The Shore Poetry – "The Winter House" and "In another universe you stay and we do each other's hair for the wedding"

storySouth – "Smooth Green Snake"

the tide rises, the tide falls – "Ocean House"

Thimble Mag – "Heist"

White Stag Publishing – "Lightning Yarn," "Pepper Bells," and "This is just to say goodbye"

Yuzu Press – "Heart Seeds"

Words and Whispers Journal – "Peat Moss'

About the Author

Sam Moe is the author of three books of poetry. Her chapbook *Animal Heart* (Harvard Square Press 2024) won second place in the International Three-Day Chapbook Contest. Her short story collection, *I Might Trust You* is forthcoming from Experiments in Fiction (Winter 2025). She has been accepted to the Sewanee Writers' Conference (2024) and received fellowships from the Longleaf Writer's Conference and the Key West Literary Seminar, and *Château d'Orquevau*. Her work has appeared or is forthcoming from *The Texas Review*, *SoFloPoJo*, *Zoetic Press*, *The Missouri Review*, and others.

FLOWERSONG
PRESS

FlowerSong Press nurtures essential verse
from, about, and throughout the borderlands.
Literary. Lyrical. Boundless.

Sign up for announcements about
new and upcoming titles at:

www.flowersongpress.com